MOM MOMENTS

*A compilation of columns from the
Northwest Indiana Times*

CARRIE STEINWEG

PublishAmerica
Baltimore

© 2011 by Carrie Steinweg.
All rights reserved. No part of this book may be reproduced, stored in a retrieval system or transmitted in any form or by any means without the prior written permission of the publishers, except by a reviewer who may quote brief passages in a review to be printed in a newspaper, magazine or journal.

First printing

PublishAmerica has allowed this work to remain exactly as the author intended, verbatim, without editorial input.

Hardcover 978-1-4626-0307-7
Softcover 978-1-4626-0308-4
PUBLISHED BY PUBLISHAMERICA, LLLP
www.publishamerica.com
Baltimore

Printed in the United States of America

Dedication

This book is dedicated to my mother, Kathryn Clark, for all the joy and laughter she's provided and sprinkled upon her family and friends through the years.

Also, to Sharon Lemming, an amazing mother of nine whom I was never able to meet face-to-face, but who inspired me through her blog and our conversations and e-mails.

Acknowledgements

These columns could not have been written had I not been blessed with the gift of motherhood. My husband, Paul, and I are lucky to have had five healthy boys that today range in age from 6 to 17. My sweet sons, Brad, Chandler, Carter, Brandon and Ian have unknowingly provided constant material with their mischief, wonder, excitement and love. My thanks to my six guys—in a house where I'm the lone female and even our dog is a male—for letting me love you unconditionally and be the matriarch of this wonderful family.

My appreciation as well to all the mothers I've known, met, interviewed or been contacted by over the years. I value your advice, admire your strength and perseverance and welcome your thoughts. I've talked to new moms, mothers with children leaving the nest and grandmothers. I've talked to mothers who have experienced miscarriage, who have lost their children to suicide and to war, who have cared for their children during chronic and debilitating illnesses, who have dealt with the pain of their children being abused, who were dying of cancer or watching their children die of cancer. I consider it a gift to have had the opportunity to be invited into their lives and from every conversation, I take a bit of them into my own role as a mother and remind myself of how truly blessed I am to have this job.

Many thanks to the editors I've worked with over the years at the Northwest Indiana Times who allowed me to share my mothering experiences and to vent and rant and reminisce—Robert Blaszkiewicz, Chrisa Zivanovic, Karin Saltanovitz, Rich Bird and Jeanette Lach.

Thank you to MaryBeth Witulski of MBW Photography for providing the cover image.

Columns contained in this book are reprinted from the Northwest Indiana Times..

As I was growing up, there were two things I always wanted to be: a mother and a writer. When I was on maternity leave with my second son, I had been sending articles and queries to editors. One day, I got an e-mail from an editor of a parenting magazine with a small assignment for an upcoming issue. I was ecstatic. I'd be able to write about something I was passionate about and get paid for it.

Over a decade later, I'm still writing. I've had something published continually in some kind of publication every month since then. Being a parent, there was so much material to emerge in an average day. So much of what I write is kid-focused and the two roles just seem to go hand-in-hand. It's sometimes hectic, but I've appreciated the opportunity to be able to share through articles and columns—and now this book—the highlights of the motherhood role and some of the topics that we all struggle with.

Not too long after that first article was published, I was working on my first book and had started doing travel writing in the Northwest Indiana Times, writing "One Tank Trip" articles. They were often family-friendly places and I focused on what parents and children would enjoy at each attraction. A few weeks later I started writing a local column, which I still write today. Sometimes the column focused on local happenings or current events, but other weeks it was all about being a mother and dealing with the unpredictable, chaotic lifestyle that often goes along with it. A few of those columns can be found in this book.

In 2005, when a regular column written by a local woman was cut from the features section, I asked my editor if I could step in and write a column on motherhood to fill that spot. He agreed and my column started running every other Sunday, alternating with a column on fatherhood by one of their regular reporters.

    I was asked by my editor to come up with a name for the column, which I pondered with much difficulty. I asked my husband. His suggestion: "I Won't Have Anything Nice for 18 Years." Ha! It was a true statement, but didn't exactly fit for a column title. I'm a fan of alliteration and Mom Moments was the first thing to pop into my mind. It didn't feel creative enough, but it did fit. I wanted my column to document the moments of being a parent that stick with you years down the road—moments that are meaningful, significant, heartfelt. I think I'm accomplishing that.

    Over the years, I've been so wrapped up in meeting deadlines, that putting entries in to journals and jotting things into baby books has fallen by the wayside. Then I realized that I have been recording memories all along in my ongoing column. The growth chart and studio photos may be absent, but in my columns there's a glimpse into the kind of mother I am, what I wish for my children, the lessons I hope to teach them. So, I hope they'll forgive me for some blank spaces in the baby book and that this collection of expressions will suffice. I also hope that those who have been readers of my column and other mothers out there who are experiencing similar rollercoaster journeys of parenthood will enjoy skimming through this sampling of my columns.

    I also invite you to visit www.nwitimes.com and search my name in the archives to view more columns and features and news articles I've written. You can also visit my website at www.carriesteinweg.com to learn more about me and follow me on Twitter (Carrieste) or look up my "Mom Moments" page on Facebook.

Another reason for tissue this season

June 7, 2002

This is the time of year when there are so many occasions that cause you to reminisce.

It's time for graduations, weddings, showers, retirements, anniversaries, reunions. It's the time of year when sentimental people like myself seriously consider buying stock in Kleenex.

Besides all of the above, my two oldest sons just celebrated birthdays.

As any parent knows, when your child celebrates a birthday it's a time when you look back in amazement and wonder, "where has the time gone?" You recall the day that the child entered the world, you reflect on all that he's accomplished up to this point and you ponder what the future will hold.

It's also the end of the school year for my older son, a time when the year is coming to a close with picnics and parties, report cards and concerts.

At a recent school musical, my eyes teared as I watched my son on stage with his classmates singing the song he'd been rehearsing in quiet corners of the house determined to keep it a "surprise." The patriotic theme only fed my weepiness as I heard little voices performing "God Bless America" and "America the Beautiful."

In addition to all the usual emotional business of the season, the recent ceremony at ground zero concluding the recovery and clean up of the site was a poignant reminder of how different the world is now as compared to last fall. As I turned on a television at work to view the ceremony, I was accompanied by one co-worker. Another later joined for a couple minutes. It wasn't like in September, when the whole office gathered to watch what was happening on the screen. I just felt like it was something I needed to watch, even if I was the only one in front of the television.

The bagpipes. The honor guard. The empty flag-draped stretcher being carried. The ringing of the fire department bell. It sent chills up my spine and tears streaming down my face.

I was soon recalling not only the birthdays of my older sons, but the day my third son was born. I was due in mid-October. As my due date approached, I thought to myself that I'd like to give birth any day except the 11th. It had been just a few short weeks since the terrorist attacks and how awful it would be to forever associate his birthdate with the one-month anniversary of that dreadful event. Selfish thought, I suppose, and not very practical. Babies are born when they're ready—not when mom decides it's most convenient or most desired.

Towards the end of my pregnancy, we were still discussing middle names for the baby. We knew it was a boy and we had selected the first name, but were still trying to come up with a suitable middle name.

The week after Sept. 11, I sat at home by myself watching the prayer service at Yankee stadium. I saw families holding photos of missing loved ones. It was devastating. One photo caught my eye. It was a large picture of a young firefighter placed on a poster board. His name was written below it—Christian.

I stopped looking for a middle name for the baby.

I'd found it.

It turned out that I spent the morning of Oct. 11 in the labor room watching President Bush request a moment of silence to remember the victims of the tragedy at the moment the second tower had fallen one month earlier.

That afternoon, my healthy baby boy was born. It was a joyful event for me in the midst of what seemed to be the whole world falling apart for others, especially that mother at Yankee stadium who held

MOM MOMENTS

the photo of her son, Christian. I think of her each time I say my son's middle name or when the calendar indicates that it's the 11th.

And, sadly, these thoughts are added this year to the flood of memories that go along with the weddings and graduations and other seasonal situations that cause me to reach for the box of tissue.

Thanks for the memories

August 9, 2002

This past week has definitely been one to remember. I hit an unwanted milestone—the end of the first three decades of my life.

I didn't have a big party to celebrate. No trip to the tavern with friends to lament the passing of my youth. The day came and went without much ado. It was probably best.

As a child, I viewed anyone over age 30 as "old."

It's difficult to now see myself in that category. Actually, the closer I've gotten to the 3-0 mark, the farther I've extended where the "old" line starts. Maybe 40, 50, 60 isn't that old, I say to myself.

Besides the trauma of turning 30, I also "retired" from my full-time job this past week. For the past 12 years I've worked in the human resources department at School District 205, the past six as the administrative assistant to the human resource director.

It's a job that I really loved, so leaving was pretty hard. Actually, I plan to work a little more from time to time until my replacement is fully trained. So, the fact that I'll still be coming and going has made it a little easier.

Some of these co-workers have known me since I was 16 and started working in the office as part of a high school work program. Some of them attended my wedding. Many of them have seen me through three pregnancies. So many of them are truly like family and I'll miss seeing their faces every day.

As in many workplaces, there's a lot of humor. Sometimes that's what you need to get you through a frustrating day. My co-workers provided quite a few laughs, just when they were needed.

MOM MOMENTS

Now that I'll no longer be employed full-time, I plan to spend more time writing. I've got a second book in the works and will continue writing on travel and family topics, but the bulk of my time will be spent being the kind of mom I always wanted to be—the kind of mom who's waiting at home after school, who spends mornings watching reruns of Sesame Street and who can run off to the park on the spur of the moment.

Juggling work and caring for kids is a complicated task. I'm looking forward to being able to schedule field trips without having to request vacation days and putting an end to bypassing home cooked meals for a bag of hamburgers because of a lack of time.

When I think about it all—the fact that I'm 30, the 12 years I spent at my job, how quickly the kids are growing up, it seems like it all happened in the blink of an eye. Sometimes things seem like they'll never change and then all of a sudden everything changes, but I guess I tend to look at life as though everything is temporary—good and bad.

The bad things become bearable when you accept that they won't last forever. The good things seem sweeter when you realize that they may not exist tomorrow. When that is your outlook on life, you learn not to let roadblocks stand in your way, but to use them as a way of making you stronger. It helps you to appreciate all that is truly worthwhile and special and makes you recognize that some of those curve balls you're thrown are blessings because in the short time that they are visible in your life, they help to shape who you are.

So, I now say goodbye to my job and my youth and look forward to my next temporary quest.

Soaking up a second language easy for kids

June 28, 2002

I heard a funny story this week that was worth sharing.

A co-worker had her grandchildren visiting recently from Puerto Rico. Her youngest daughter was raised in Riverdale and met and married a fellow doctor. The two now live in Puerto Rico with their children, who speak both English and Spanish.

While visiting, the oldest of the grandchildren, who is 4 years old, was riding in a car with her aunt when they were involved in a minor traffic accident. It turned out that the individual who hit them was a woman who did not speak English, only Spanish. The 4-year-old ended up serving as a translator to her aunt and police. It makes for great bragging material for a grandmother.

Besides the good chuckle I got, I also found the story interesting because my 8-year-old son is taking a summer class in beginning Spanish, so I'm sure he'll soon be rattling off far more Spanish words and phrases than I know.

In high school I took one year of Spanish and, of course, I now regret not taking another year or two. Like so many other things that we adults cram into our heads, if you don't use it—and right away—it's likely lost forever.

Now I recognize how useful it could have been to spend more time learning another language. And Spanish is a language that is so common in today's society. I would have had many opportunities to communicate with others who speak the language on a daily basis.

A few years ago, I remember reading a newspaper article about an elementary school that I believe was in Chicago Heights, where Spanish was taught in kindergarten. I remember being so impressed that these children were being given the opportunity to learn another language at the optimum time in their lives to retain it.

Most children do not have the opportunity to enroll in language classes until high school, or in some cases junior high. While a teenager can usually easily grasp a new language without problem, research has shown that early elementary school, or earlier, is the best time to introduce a second language to a child.

I have an uncle who was born and raised in Europe. He speaks several languages. His early years were spent in Spain, so Spanish was the first language he learned. However, he learned English, German, and Portuguese at an early age. Having the ability to speak more than one language afforded him so many opportunities. As a teacher in the United States, he was often able to communicate easily with students who were not fluent in English or had difficulties in communicating because English was their second language. He and my aunt have traveled all over the world and being able to communicate in other languages provided him a great advantage as a tourist.

I'm enjoying the review in Spanish as I study with my son. Hopefully, the small portion of the language that he learns in his six-week course will stay with him—or better yet, perhaps it will motivate him to learn more about that language or perhaps he'll be a better translator than I am.

Blame it on the Third Child syndrome

December 20, 2002

These days it seems new diseases and conditions are being discovered every time you turn around.

Or there are medical breakthroughs that help bring about treatments for those who suffer from serious ailments. Every once in a while you hear about an ailment and wonder if it's a condition that can really be considered a "disease" or if it's a flimsy excuse for a flaw in one's lifestyle or personality.

Recently, I heard a term that perfectly explains my faults and gives me something to blame them on.

I was groaning to my friend Amy how I never seemed to have time to do things I used to. I told her how my reliable memory was failing me and how I never seem to get around to sending birthday and anniversary cards as I faithfully had done in the past.

"It's the Third Child syndrome," she explained. "You're pretty good after the first one and you slip a little after the second one, but after the third one—forget it."

She went on to describe the symptoms (lack of hours in the day, short- and long-term memory loss, loss of order in one's life, decrease in creativity, etc.), all of which I seem to suffer from. I no longer needed to feel guilty. There was a medical explanation for everything that seemed to be falling to the wayside.

MOM MOMENTS

Amy was speaking from experience. She's the mom of three and I've known her since long before she was married and had kids. She'd definitely get my vote for mom of the year. However, once I thought about it, I realized that she too had been a victim of this common condition.

Amy is one of those amazingly talented and crafty people. Every year we would get a homemade ornament enclosed in our Christmas card. That doesn't happen anymore now that she's the mom of three.

She can also sew wonderfully. When I became a mother, she presented me with a shirt that had "MOM" affixed to it. She'd cut out the letters from material that her mother had used to sew some of her clothes when she was a child. She paid so much attention to every detail. When my second son was born, she also had two children, but somehow managed to sew an amazing quilt for my baby. By the time I had my third child, her third was toddling around. Instead of a handmade item, she presented my son with an adorable outfit—but it was made by Carter's, not by Amy.

We used to get together for homemade dinners, but now we see each other pretty much only when one of our kids has a birthday. The homemade dinners have been replaced by buckets of chicken and catered meals. Although she manages to still do things that would send most moms spinning, that Third Child syndrome seems to have hit her, too.

Wow, if Amy could be stricken with this syndrome anyone could, I thought. I'll bet that one morning in the near future, I'll turn on Oprah and find a panel of moms of three speaking about the subject.

Seriously, though, it's just a comical indication of how crazy our lives get when we have a gang of kids to care for, but it's just funny how true it is.

There was one trait that my family always seemed to envy about me. I used to be organized. I had a great memory. I had a mental calendar of the birthdays of my parents, five siblings, their spouses and their children, my in-laws and my co-workers. I'd have a birthday gift bought and wrapped at least a month in advance. I never missed sending a birthday card—and they always arrived on time, or earlier. Whenever I received a gift, a thank you was in the mail within three or four days. My Christmas cards were usually ordered in August and addressed by late October or early November. I almost always mailed them the week of Thanksgiving, so that they'd be the first to arrive. I took the first two children for professional photos every six to 12 weeks for the first two years of their lives.

Needless to say, that description of me is a thing of the past.

Just as Amy said, I barely missed a beat after my first child. Even after my second, there wasn't really a noticeable change. But now that I've had my third, it's all over.

I still remember birthdays, but usually not until they've passed. Gifts often arrive late and are thrown in a recycled gift bag on the way out the door. My thank you notes are usually sent via e-mail and sometimes take a few weeks to arrive. At 14-months-old, my third child has only been photographed professionally four times. Still, not bad, but if you saw my first child's photo album, you'd understand why it's a sad failure. And, here we are—less than a week away from Christmas and most of my cards have yet to make it out the door. Of the 200-plus cards that I usually send out, I probably have 170 to go. So, if you usually get a Christmas card from the Steinweg family and it hasn't arrived yet, don't worry—it will, but it may be into the new year before it gets there.

Sorry, but it's not my fault. That darned Third Child syndrome is to blame.

Thinking pink the fourth time around

January 31, 2003

While it isn't unusual for flu symptoms to show up this time of year, the nausea, fatigue and aches I've had the past few weeks are symptoms of something a little more permanent than a 24-hour virus.

Baby number four will be arriving this summer.

Since I'm already the mom of three boys, I'm naturally envisioning pink blankets and booties for this one.

When most people find out that I'm expecting, the first thing they ask is if I'm going to find out the sex. It's funny to hear the different reactions from people when they discover you're pregnant. When I was pregnant with my first child, most people offered their congratulations. My enthusiasm was contagious and most people simply shared in my excitement.

When I was expecting my second child, who was due just after my first child's fifth birthday, individuals responded with, "Well, it's about time!" People couldn't seem to understand that we actually wanted that big of a span between the kids. We were completely content with our family of three for a long time.

When we were ready for another one, we had one. But as any parent knows, everyone you come into contact with during a pregnancy is intent on offering bits of advice and opinions.

Just before my second son turned two years old, we learned that we would be having another one. The third time, response had shifted from, "It's about time!" to "Again! Already!" Now people thought that it was too soon to be having another. Those who didn't comment on the time element asked, "Was it an accident?"

Now, with a fourth one on the way, which is due two and a half months shy of my youngest son's second birthday, everyone I encounter wants to know the sex of the new baby. Some people don't even realize that it isn't apparent on an ultrasound until a good ways into the pregnancy and want to know if I've found out already.

Then of course, a few people add in, "Not another one," "You're pretty brave," or "You're nuts!"

If the sex is easily apparent on the ultrasound screen, I'm sure I'll ask the technician to clue me in. With my first child, we decided to wait until delivery to find out the sex and it did add an extra element of excitement to the whole experience.

I'm just not that patient anymore. With the other two, we found out well in advance that they would be boys. Due to the fact that the suspense will drive me crazy, paired with the practical aspect of being able to prepare more easily, I'd like to find out the sex of the next child in advance. If it's a boy, I'll be all set. If it's a girl, I can start sorting through the newborn outfits, eliminating the blue and adding some pastels.

I've become so accustomed to raising boys that I'm not sure I'd even know what to do with a girl. Boys are absolutely wonderful and I'll love this child with all my heart, whether it's a boy or a girl.

But, I have to admit that it would be nice to have another female in the family. Right now I'm outnumbered four to one—make that five to one if you count the dog.

Appreciating Mom's old fashioned ways

May 9, 2003

When I was growing up, many of the other kids seemed to have hip, young moms. My mom, who gave birth to me a week shy of her 37th birthday and then had twins at age 39, seemed ancient to me.

As a teenager, of course, it was kind of a drag to have a mom in her 50s. Now that I'm a mom myself, I realize how different life would have been to have had a much younger mom.

I've been giving it a lot of thought as Mother's Day is approaching and I've come to appreciate how nice it was to have an "old-fashioned" mother as I was growing up.

In the 1970s, it was still pretty uncommon for women to be having babies in their late 30s. Many of the mothers of my friends married in their teens and early 20s and quickly began their families.

Women did not make up the huge portion of the professional work world that they do today, putting off marriage and family for careers; however, it was a time when many moms were going back to work and kids were coming home to empty houses. There were also a lot of kids I knew who were being raised by a single parent or whose parents were divorced and shared custody.

As I said earlier, our family was more old-fashioned. My dad worked and my mother stayed home with us. That is, at least until the financial demands of having three teenage daughters caused her to find a job.

When she finally went to work for the first time in many years, she worked the night shift at a convenience store so that she could sleep while we were at school and would be awake in the evenings.

In the years that she worked there, she endured many scary and odd occurrences. She received countless prank phone calls, was robbed at gunpoint, saw a car drive through the front of the store, received bomb threats and witnessed some pretty distasteful acts.

After a flasher visited the store and the police came in to make the report, the officer asked her for a description. She was so shocked by the incident, she admitted to the officer that she couldn't give much of a description above the waist.

Another of her old-fashioned qualities is that she never drove and still doesn't. She said that she tried to learn how to drive as a teen, but was afraid to make turns.

On her last venture behind the wheel, at about age 17, she drove through town in her brother's old car, which had a rumble seat where he was seated. Each time he advised her to turn, she ignored him and proceeded straight. Finally, rather than turn when the street came to a dead end, she drove into a cornfield. Whenever we went anywhere as kids, my dad chauffeured us or we walked.

Mom had many other qualities that made her old-fashioned. She thought girls were meant to wear frilly dresses. I remember going to my first day of kindergarten wearing a full-length floral dress. I could have passed for Laura Ingalls Wilder.

In the disco days, my parents would not have dreamed of listening to anything but classical music. If we weren't listening to Beethoven or Bach, we'd be treated to a few country tunes, which dad was opposed to, but my mom liked. I remember how excited my sisters and I became when we got our first non-classical record. It was by the Oak Ridge Boys.

At an early age, I remember memorizing every nursery rhyme in existence. Mom liked to read and liked to recite rhymes for us. She often revised the rhymes with silly words or inserted our names. I grew up actually thinking there was a nursery rhyme that went, "Carrie, Carrie pudding and pie, kissed the boys and made them cry."

MOM MOMENTS

Mom also liked to sing and although I love her dearly, I must say she can't carry a tune; however, it made things fun. She sang to us as we did things around the house. And although I can't carry a tune either, I enjoy singing to, and with, my little boys, thanks to her influence.

We always considered mom's cooking style to also be old-fashioned. She was raised by parents who had lived through the Great Depression. She was from a family of six. She learned to cook from her own mom, who often had to make do with very little for a family of eight.

I remember her making us a snack of bread topped with butter and sprinkled with sugar and preparing dinners of potato soup made with just potatoes, milk, water and salt. We always liked the foods she made, but noticed how other kids were eating fruit rollups or Doritos for snacks and were eating McDonald's or microwave meals for dinner, so the foods she served seemed strange to us.

She encouraged us to play outside on summer days and told us about games she'd play when she was little—and those were the days when you could play in your neighborhood from sunup until sundown without parents being terrified of their child being abducted.

Everything about my mom always seemed old-fashioned. She wasn't hurried like the other mothers I knew. She wasn't concerned about trends. She wasn't in competition with the other moms. She raised us in a slower-paced world.

And although there were plenty of times that I wasn't thrilled about my mom's lack of style or her old-fashioned behavior, I couldn't be more thankful for it now.

Savoring the final weeks of pregnancy

May 16, 2003

It's getting closer and closer now and I'm counting down the weeks. Less than ten to go now until I have my fourth son.

Any woman who has been through it will tell you that this final stage of pregnancy can be uncomfortable and tiring, but knowing this baby will be my last one has caused mixed feelings.

Of course, I'll be very excited when the baby finally arrives and a few weeks from now—especially when we hit those hot summer days—I know I'll be anxious to get it over with, but I know how much I'll miss it also.

I don't really want it to end. There's just nothing that can explain how it feels to have a baby squirming and kicking and moving around inside you. I've only got a couple months of that left and then I'll never experience it again.

If my pregnancies and deliveries were a breeze and if I was lucky enough to win the lottery, I'd love to have even more babies. But unfortunately, carrying and delivering children is not that easy and I don't have a million dollars to my name, so we're calling it quits.

This last pregnancy seems to have been the most challenging of them. For about five months I had morning sickness just about every day. I felt absolutely miserable and spent many days laying around on the sofa and getting up only when I absolutely had to. By the time it subsided, I already had made it into the third trimester and along with that came the backaches, shortness of breath, heartburn, and insomnia, not to mention the wobbly walk. So much for that "honeymoon of pregnancy" that is supposed to occur during the second trimester.

I realize how very lucky I am to have had three sons and to be expecting another. They were all born with ten fingers and ten toes and are healthy, active little boys. And my family has evolved into what I always pictured, for the most part.

First, I always wanted to have four children and here I am with my fourth one on the way. Secondly, I always wanted to have my children when I was young and vowed that I wouldn't have children in my thirties. My last child should arrive just days before I turn 31. And lastly, I guess I always expected to have two boys and two girls. That didn't work out, but two out of three isn't bad. As I said, I'm very lucky to have the beautiful, healthy boys I have.

Yet, even though my family has progressed just as I wanted, there's just that little part of me that is having a hard time accepting that this is it. I'm sure I'll get over it once the baby is here. I'll have to. I'll be too busy concentrating on how to keep him from getting any bigger.

Selecting a baby name is a difficult decision

July 11, 2003

When a couple is expecting a child, they find themselves with many decisions to make. Some are harder than others.

What will the theme of the nursery be? Which doctor will you see for prenatal care? Which hospital or birthing center will be chosen? Or will it be a home birth? Will you opt for pain relief during labor? Will the baby be bottle-fed or breastfed? Do you want the baby to "room in" or spend more time in the nursery while you rest? Will you find out the sex of the baby? If it's a boy, will he be circumcised? Will you take advantage of tests available during the pregnancy? How much time will you take off work after the birth or will you return to work at all after the baby is born? Will you bank your baby's umbilical cord blood? Will you attend Lamaze classes? Will you prepare a birth plan to follow? Who will be in the delivery room?

There's a lot to think about when you've got a baby on the way. Since I'm expecting my fourth child, most of these decisions are not a big issue. I've been through it before and I know, for the most part, what to expect—although childbirth is full of surprises. Most of these decisions were just a given—a repeat of the previous pregnancy. Some didn't require a lot of thought or much debate.

However, the one decision that has been the most difficult this time around is selecting a name for the baby. With this being the fourth child, it doesn't seem like it should be a decision that would be that difficult. After naming three boys and knowing in advance that the next child is a boy, it should be easy, right?

By now, we should know what style of name we like. You'd think we might have a reserve of close finalists from previous pregnancies to pull from, but we don't. With each of the other boys, we had the first name decided far in advance. All three times, the middle name was decided pretty late in the game or even reconsidered or changed after birth, but coming up with a first name was easy. This time around, there wasn't one name that we were set on from early on, as was the case with each of the other pregnancies.

Many parents select names that all have the same initials, that rhyme or that all have the same amount of syllables. We didn't follow that road. Well each name has two syllables, but that was coincidence, not planned. It's not a problem of finding a name that's acceptable, it's more finding a name my husband and I can agree on. There are several names that I like that he doesn't care for. The ones that he seems to like, I'm not crazy about. So sometime before the baby arrives, or shortly after, we're going to have to come up with some kind of compromise.

When I'm asked if we've chosen the name yet, I just say that we're still undecided. I've learned from experience what happens when you reveal the name beforehand. Everyone has an opinion and sometimes those opinions make you second-guess your choice. With my first and second pregnancies, I remember hearing criticism about some of the names I was considering. The third time around, I didn't spill the beans until he arrived, except to a very few people who I didn't think would throw their two cents in, even if they didn't like it.

Selecting a name isn't something that can be taken lightly. It is truly something that will affect the child for the rest of his life. There are plenty of adults who have not been pleased with their parents' choice in naming them, but even a mother and father who named their son Francis or Bubba, did so with good intentions, I'm sure.

So, during the next couple of weeks, I'll be pondering that one big decision. I'll be trying to convince my husband that my favorite names are better than the ones he's leaning toward and hoping that when our child is 30 years old, he won't think we were crazy for coming up with the name we settle on.

Boys will be boys...and monkeys and apes and other wild animals

September 6, 2003

"Are you ready?" I hear my nine-year-old call out from the other room.

"You want a piece of me?" his younger brother answers, followed by "You're going down!"

A series of thumps and crashes can be heard and I run to intervene before someone is in tears or bleeding.

No matter how I've tried to eliminate this kind of rough and rowdy behavior in my boys, I've realized my efforts are useless. Kids will be kids and boys will be boys.

Growing up among sisters, I wasn't prepared to have children who played so rough. I was used to tea parties and dressing up dolls. Sure, my sisters and I fought from time to time, but it was usually over a toy or piece of clothing and would begin as a game of tug of war and end with a girly slap or hair pulling. We'd then sit in separate corners and pout.

Through my first son's toddler and preschool years, I always emphasized playing gentle and being kind. And, with him being my first, I usually avoided activities that might result in him getting dirty or getting a bruise or a scratch on the knee. I hovered over him so closely that if I saw him expressing even a hint of aggression, I'd try to correct his behavior and/or remove him from the situation. Even with his mother stifling him to prevent any violent or rough acts, his boyish tendencies came through.

Once his little brother came along, and as soon as he could crawl, the two would tumble and wrestle on the floor. They'd bang on their chests and howl and imitate Tarzan. And as time went on they'd get rougher and rougher.

Fast forward to the third boy. He's now 21-months-old and just as tough as the other two. After witnessing plenty of wrestling matches on the living room floor, he jumps right in when the other two go at it. It always starts out as fun, with all of them laughing. Nine times out of ten, though, somebody ends up getting squished or getting knocked down or getting bumped harder than he expected.

I'm starting to become immune to all the thumps and bangs I hear, but I usually shudder for a few seconds anticipating a bleeding lip, a sprained wrist or a black eye. There just aren't any tea parties when you're raising a house full of boys.

Conversations with a Three-Year-Old

September 13, 2003

Parents love to hear their baby's babbles and coos. What sound could be sweeter than the voice of your child?

What's really remarkable to me is how in such a short time, a child can go from being virtually unable to communicate verbally, other than by crying, to forming complete sentences, imitating the tones and inflections of adults around them and carrying on a legitimate two-sided conversation.

With a son who turned three recently, I find myself just awestruck at how quickly he picks up words and phrases and how easily he repeats them. I'd like to think he's genius material, but the fact is that by age three, most children have logged hundreds of words into their heads that become part of their everyday vocabulary. Some of my son's statements at this age strike me so funny. I figured I should write some of them down. Here's a sample of how a few conversations have gone.

Conversation No. 1:
Son: Mom, lets make some Kool-aid.
Mom: Ok, what kind?
Son: The Magic Twist kind. It's green.
Mom: (Opening up the container) No, honey, it's yellow.
Son: It's green.
Mom: It says it's strawberry flavored, but it's yellow.
Son: No, it's green.

MOM MOMENTS

(We proceed to add the water and Mom realizes that Magic Twist Kool-aid changes color when you add water. As we added water, it turned green.)
Mom: Oh, it is green.
Son: See, it's green!
Mom: All done. Want a glass?
Son: Yeah, Mom. You did a good job.
Conversation No. 2:
(I'm driving. My son is seated in his car seat in the back of the van. I'm sipping from a can of soda.)
Son: Mom!!!! Stop!!!!
(I screech to a halt in the middle of the street)
Mom: What's wrong?
Son: You can't drink and drive!
Conversation No. 3:
(The two of us are watching television and the show breaks for commercial. A commercial for cat litter comes on.)
Son: Do you want to get that Mom?
Mom: But we don't have a cat.
Son: You need to get that.
(A commercial comes on for shampoo)
Son: Mom, do you want to get that?
Mom: No, Mommy uses a different kind of shampoo.
Son: But you need to get that.
(The show resumes. At the next break, a commercial comes on for a prescription medication for high-blood pressure.)
Son: Mom, do you want to get that?
Mom: No, that's medicine. Mommy doesn't need that.
Son: You need to get that.
(Later in the day, another commercial comes on for a hair accessory kit)
Son: Mom, do you want that?
Mom: Maybe Mommy can get that sometime.
Son: I'll put it on your Christmas list.

Welcoming two new additions

September 20, 2003

As I'm sitting at the computer to type this column, I've got a newborn napping in the other room and a stack of papers by my side.

Although I'm yawning and feeling drowsy, I've got work to do. Just as occurred after giving birth to my other sons, I spent the first few days on a high, unable to rest because of the excitement. I'd be up late feeding the baby and by the time I got him settled and got myself comfortable, he'd be awake again or ready to eat again.

So, I spent several days managing on as little as three or four hours of sleep, (and that was usually broken up into 20- or 30-minute increments) but it really didn't bother me. Now it's catching up with me. After a few weeks of it, I'm getting worn out.

We've recently welcomed our fourth baby home and it's been quite an adjustment. The first days at home were wonderful. The baby slept quite a bit in the first few days.

The older boys were ecstatic to have a new baby brother. They all wanted to help and all wanted to hold the baby. As the days have gone by, the boys are still excited to have the baby here, but are getting tired of hearing me ask them to be patient and wait until I'm done tending to the baby.

Along with our new son, I have another new arrival to celebrate. My second book recently came out. The book is a pictorial history of the village of South Holland, published by Arcadia Publishing, and is similar to my first book, which was on Lansing. The details of its arrival are amusing, so I thought I'd share the story.

This past spring, I was looking forward to the baby's arrival and had sent off the final materials to my publisher in May, expecting it to be available in late August. I was tickled when I looked at the publisher's Web site and saw the book was due out the same day the baby was due.

I called my dad and told him what I'd discovered. We laughed and wondered which would arrive first, the baby or the book.

As the due date for the baby grew closer, I worried that he was going to be stubborn about making his entrance. I worried about having to be induced. And I worried about having the baby get too large due to the gestational diabetes I'd been diagnosed with and having that require me to have another Caesarean section.

It surprised me when I woke up on the morning that the baby and the book were due and I was having contractions. By the time I arrived at the doctor's office later that morning for my scheduled appointment, the contractions were weaker and less frequent and had almost stopped completely. When I had a non-stress test done in the office, the baby was moving, but there were no contractions.

I went home feeling a bit disappointed. I was ready for the baby to arrive, even if he wasn't ready. When I got home, my husband occupied the boys so that I could take a nap. When I woke up a short time later, the contractions were back and much stronger and more frequent. Since I didn't have a history of quick labors, I procrastinated.

"I'll go to the hospital when they are a little stronger or a little closer together," I thought.

When I realized that I needed to start heading to the hospital, I started to gather my things. I heard a knock at the door. I waddled to the door and opened it. My book was arriving—right on its due date. And it looked like the baby was also going to arrive on its due date, but actually he didn't.

We got to the hospital a little before 6 p.m. and we thought he'd surely get there by midnight, but he held out until an hour and a half into the next day. So the book arrived on time and the baby almost did.

I guess the book won the race by about eight hours.

Looking for some motherly advice?

October 18, 2003

Let me start by saying that I'm not a child-care expert. I'm not a pediatrician. I don't have a degree in child development. I'm far from being qualified as a child psychologist.

However, I've been a parent for nearly 10 years now and have four children, which gives me the feeling that I know enough about child rearing to offer some bits of motherly advice. So for those new or soon to be parents, here are some tips from an experienced mom:

When changing a baby boy's diaper, do not leave him exposed for more than 1/100th of a second. You'll be sorry if you do.

Always buy white grape juice. Only buy purple grape juice if you have a purple rug and purple furniture.

Be a good role model and force yourself to eat Brussels sprouts once in a while.

Don't be afraid to act weird or silly. Your children won't think any less of you.

Don't purchase clothing for your children that is white.

Don't purchase clothing for yourself that is white, either. They'll manage to stain it, too.

Even if they seem interested, NO ONE is interested in hearing about the contents of your child's diaper. Please spare everyone the details.

MOM MOMENTS

Don't compare your child to others when it comes to milestones, such as walking and talking. Hard to do I know, but it'll drive you nuts. Let them take their time and enjoy the stage their in.

Rent the movie "Parenthood," starring Steve Martin.

On the first day of school, wait until you get back to the car to start sobbing.

Write names and dates on the back of all your photographs!!! (Advice from my own mother, who said I'd never be able to tell which of my children was which in photographs because they all look so much alike. She was right.)

Don't cry over spilled milk (or cereal or peas or pudding or rice or mashed potatoes or spaghetti sauce or any other messy food they find to drop or throw.) Everything is washable.

Write everything down or you'll forget it. With each child that you give birth to, you lose a few more brain cells. Both your short and long-term memory should be shot before your second child turns one.

Record milestones and special memories in the baby book. When something special happens you think you'll never forget it, but it'll slip through your mind before you know it. When she gets older, she'll appreciate reading what your thoughts were on the day she was born or knowing how old she was when she got her first tooth.

Even if you're deathly afraid of spiders or some other insect or animal, contain yourself, unless you want to see your son running around in circles with his arms flailing and screaming like a girl. Everything you do rubs off on them.

When your children begin picking their own outfits, be prepared for them to dress as if they're color blind.

Never let them go to bed without a kiss and a hug.

Don't let them run with scissors, There's a reason your parents told you not to!

Try not to let it get to you when you find yourself awake with an energetic or sick child at 3 a.m. All too soon you'll find yourself in an empty house wishing you had a little one to keep you awake.

This year, think and be thankful

November 22, 2003

Turkey and stuffing. Cranberry sauce and pumpkin pie.

The menu items are probably the first things that come to mind at the mention of Thanksgiving.

Beyond the much anticipated calorie loaded meal, it's a time of year when a reality check is in order. It's a time to think about all the blessings that take place in our lives everyday that often go unnoticed or unappreciated. It's a time to reflect on what we're truly grateful for. And it's a time to forget about material possessions and be thankful for the people that are part of our lives and the special little things that we share with them that make life worth living.

So, as Thanksgiving approaches, I spent a little time thinking about some of the things that I'm grateful for—even the littlest things. Here's what I came up with:

I'm thankful for the sunny days
Spent playing in the toasty rays
For footsteps thumping in the hall
And WASHABLE crayon drawn on my wall
For wheels that get me here and there
For shoes on my feet, so they don't go bare
For clothes on my back, a roof over my head
Running hot water and comfortable bed
Fannie May candies, irresistible sweets

MOM MOMENTS

Snickers, Milky Ways and all chocolate treats
Soldiers at home, far away and at sea
Working to keep us each safe and free
For flowers growing in the Spring
For bunnies hopping, birds that sing
For Mom's phone calls, Daddy's hugs
Caterpillars and lighting bugs
Little arms that hold me tight
Babies to cuddle with late at night
A beating heart and eyes that see
And angels watching over me
Animal crackers, macaroni and cheese
Little boys who say "thank you" and "please"
Birthday wishes that do come true
A kiss on the cheek out of the blue
Dirty faces and sticky hands
Crazy glue and rubber bands
Nursery rhymes and baseball cards
Sand boxes and back yards
Things don't always go my way
But I shouldn't let it rule the day
There's so much to appreciate
And tomorrow it could be too late
So thanks for all favors, big and small
From everybody, one and all
For all the things that I hold dear
Every day throughout the year

Feeling old? Got bubbles?

December 6, 2003

Somehow as we're thrown into the adult world, we lose sight of so many simple pleasures.

All of the responsibilities in our lives leave us feeling hurried and stressed and too busy to notice and appreciate little things. And once those rose-colored glasses and naive senses are lost, it's hard—sometimes impossible—to regain them.

However, for parents, there is an opportunity to briefly escape to that wonderful world of childhood when you didn't care what time the clock said and you could spend hours completely entertained by sitting on a sidewalk with a pile of sticks and rocks.

Having a child is the perfect excuse to be able to play again. How else would a mature adult be able to justify hopping on a toboggan and sliding down a hill or filling a Super Soaker and engaging in water battle? It's okay when your offspring are present.

Try to do it alone and you'll undoubtedly get some funny looks.

Somehow our little ones are able to help transport us back to a time when it was fun to jump on beds and make snow angels. Sure we may still complain when we have to straighten out the bedspread or when we soak our bottoms as we lie down in the snow, but the enjoyment temporarily outweighs the inconvenience. For the moment, when we're bouncing in mid-air surrounded by pillows or swishing in the fresh flakes of a snowfall, the bills, the dishes and the deadlines just fade away, if only for a few seconds.

MOM MOMENTS

I had one of those euphoric experiences recently on one of our unseasonably warm days. While his older brother was at school and the little ones napped, my four-year-old and I spent some time out in the back yard. Armed with a juice box and a shovel, he headed for the sandbox. After a few minutes, he requested some more digging equipment and we made our way into the garage, where he came across a giant bubble wand that had been sitting in a drawer since last year.

"Let's get my bubbles," he cried, barely able to contain his excitement. He jumped up and down as if he were in a long line to use a public washroom. A few minutes later we were all set up with a plate full of the sudsy liquid and an instrument designed to make the biggest bubbles you've ever seen.

For the next hour or so, the rest of the world disappeared. Me my little boy and our bubbles were the only things that mattered. We took turns blowing them. Then we took turns chasing them and trying to pop them. Then we spun is circles watching the bubbles chase us. It was just the kind of mindless activity that I needed and the smile on my son's face told me that he enjoyed our time together as much as I did.

Would I have ever retrieved the bubbles and the wand on my own? Not a chance. But with my little guy to guide me, I was able to rediscover the simple pleasure of blowing bubbles. So next time you're having a bad day, grab your child and a bottle of bubbles and have a ball. And even if you don't have a little one around, give it a try. I won't tell anyone!

Another holiday bites the dust

January 1, 2004

I'm writing this column just a couple hours after the last guests have left our holiday celebration.

After all the weeks of shopping and wrapping and baking and sending cards, it's suddenly over.

The initial thought is often relief that things can now slow down, but it's usually followed by a sad disappointment that the excitement and magic of the holidays is also gone. I think many parents pause after the celebrations and wonder how their children will remember the holiday and realize how fleeting these special moments are.

I was doing just that as these lines came to mind, so I'll share my sappy rhyme. Hope you're holidays were very merry.

'Twas the night after Christmas and all through the house
Were toys and boxes and my new gray striped blouse
Scattered about the living room without care
Were bits of wrapping and bows just lying there
When from the living room I heard such a clatter
I put down the dishes to see what was the matter
'Twas only the dog sitting on a talking stuffed elf
So I picked him up and placed him up on a shelf
Beside him were candles and breakables and
Other items placed far from the 2-year-olds hands
On Gameboy and Leap pad and electronic devices

MOM MOMENTS

Went up to the counter near the crystal and spices
Next to the tree, were the toys all in stacks
Karaoke and Legos and train cars for tracks
Some blocks for the baby, some candy for me
"I can play by myself," I whispered with glee.
So onto the keyboard my fingers then sped
While Elvis and Beatles tunes hummed in my head
I pulled out the race cars and played with the track
And went to the fridge for a sweet midnight snack
I sighed with relief, it was done for the year
Then what to my wondering eyes did appear?
A photo of a cute little read head boy
Who next year will ask for a big-kid toy
A shot of a baby with a smile on his face
Who next Christmas will be walking all over the place
A four year old who wants to be just like big brother
But is still small enough to cuddle with mother
And the oldest boy, at the age of nine
May not believe in Santa next time
I sat by myself, not making a sound
They'll all be older the next time around
They're growing and growing at every sight
So, I'll go to their beds and kiss them goodnight
And whisper into each tiny ear
"Merry Christmas, my sweetheart, until next year."

The neighborhood changed forever when Mr. Rogers died

January 3, 2004

As one year comes to a close and another begins, the events of the past year are replayed on news shows or recounted on the front pages.

Each year I enjoy looking back at what's happened over the past year. By year's end, many of the events of the early months have escaped our minds and it often seems like much longer than a year since they occurred.

The first things that came to mind before watching all the highlights of 2003 on television were the capture of Saddam Hussein and the outstanding season that the Cubs had. Sure there was a lot more that went on last year, but those are two things I'm sure I'll recall years down the road.

In addition to the rundown of the news events of the past year, you see a lot about the people who died during the year. That's something that intrigues me more than what happened.

Again, the more recent deaths, like Paul Simon, probably are the first that people in the area might think of. However there were great entertainers, politicians, athletes, and others that died earlier in the year that we don't easily recall.

Each of those people left something behind, something the public will remember them for. Because they were enjoyed on the television screen, we remember them for their obvious talents.

MOM MOMENTS

I spoke to my father on the phone on New Year's Eve after he watched a television show about famous people who died in 2003. He rattled off the names of people that I'd forgotten about, like Bob Hope and Kathrine Hepburn. We brought up the names of John Ritter and Johnny Cash, Gregory Hines and Nell Carter.

There was one person that was lost in 2003 that really saddened me and since I didn't get around to writing anything about it at the time of his death, I thought I'd do it now. That person was Fred Rogers.

During my childhood, PBS was the channel to turn on for programming for young kids. There was no Nickelodeon, Disney Channel or Cartoon Channel. Since attending preschool was not yet the norm, children under age five learned a lot from PBS and shows like Mr. Rogers, Sesame Street and Electric Company.

Other than what was taught to preschoolers by their parents, it was exposure to these shows that prepared them for kindergarten. They learned their numbers watching Electric Company, their alphabet while viewing Sesame Street and from Mr. Rogers they learned about feelings, friends, neighbors and feeding fish, with a few other lessons on life thrown in.

I must have watched quite a bit of Mr. Rogers as a young child, so much so that I was inclined to write him a letter. I was elated when I got a response and an autographed picture. Mr. Rogers had a way of making children feel special and receiving his letter and picture in the mail made my day.

I watch reruns now with my own children, and while the shows may seem lame to some children today in comparison to other children's programming, he still strikes a chord with young viewers and conveys messages that are important. The land of make believe may lack the excitement of the Powerpuff Girls or Pokemon, but who would have thought that a middle-aged man singing while he tied his shoes and put on a sweater would captivate audiences the way he did? He's someone who made quite an impact and he and his neighborhood and his catchy theme song are missed.

Bullying shouldn't happen in our schools

February 7, 2004

I often write my column on lighthearted topics or humorous happenings, but this week I wanted to tackle something a little more serious. (And no, it's not about the Super bowl half-time show. Although it was extremely distasteful, everyone has heard enough about it.)

I was doing some research on the Internet and came across a Web site about a National No Name-Calling Week that takes place March 1-5. It's an effort to decrease bullying in schools.

On the site, http://www.glsen.org/cgi-bin/iowa/noname/about.html, it explains the idea for this project came from a book by author James Howe, called "The Misfits," which is about a group of four seventh-graders who are repeatedly harassed and who run for student government with a platform to wipe out name calling. I haven't read the book, but it's a topic I know that many young students could identify with.

Name calling and bullying has occurred in every school to some extent. Any parent, teacher or administrator that would argue otherwise is extremely naive. In my own days as a student and in my interactions with students now that my kids are in school, I've witnessed it in kids as young as age four.

Two incidents of bullying that I heard about this week reminded me of how far this bullying can go sometimes. One was a situation that was highlighted on "Good Morning America." A high school student had been bullied at school and had even had her picture posted on a Web site as the "ugliest girl in the school." After living with the harassment for quite some time without an effort on the part of school officials to stop it, her mother, a lawyer, sued the school district and was awarded a settlement. When the girl was shown on television, she was far from ugly. She was an attractive, blond girl with a pretty face and a bright smile. She eventually changed schools and was in a completely different environment; free from the daily bullying she'd received at her old school.

The second incident I heard about involved a 13-year-old Hammond girl who was "pushed from behind and slammed into the wall. The impact broke both of her arms, her wrist and her glasses," as reported in a Times article.

The offender initially received only a three-day suspension. The punishment was later extended to a ten-day suspension. The mother argued that the punishment was not severe enough. She wanted her daughter's attacker expelled.

I'd have to agree with the mother. Had the attacker been an adult who had done the same thing, she would have been arrested for battery. And how can this victim return to school, where she'll have to face her attacker again on a daily basis?

Bullying has been a hot topic in recent years. Since the tragedy at Columbine High School in 1999, in which two students who had been described at "outcasts" and "nerds" and were victims of bullying, killed 12 students and a teacher, the topic has been taken very seriously. Other school shootings followed and there seemed to be a pattern of students who were victims of bullying acting out violently in response.

However, an outcome such as the Columbine tragedy is rare. Many children who are bullied suffer in silence. Often they are afraid to tell anyone for fear of the bullying getting worse.

This is one topic I can talk about from experience. I remember being bullied pretty much from the time I started school.

Each day when I walked to school, which was a block away, a boy from my neighborhood would follow behind me. All the way to school, he'd call me names. Sometimes he'd pick up sticks and poke me in the back as I walked. Sometimes he'd throw rocks at me as I walked.

I was a timid little girl and never told any adults about what was happening. And honestly, in those days, I'm not sure how much good it would have done. While adults may not have approved of the behavior, it may have been shrugged off as "kids being kids."

Besides, the way I was brought up, problems were not always dealt with, but often ignored. My parents were raised in an era when secrets and uncomfortable situations were often swept under the rug, rather than being exposed in front of the world on Jerry Springer, or they were fed the unrealistic notion that any problem could be solved with a glass of mom's milk and cookies or one of Dad's pep talks in less than thirty minutes, as in the Cleaver home on "Leave it To Beaver." I guess I learned early on not to be aggressive or confrontational, but that also made me an easy target for all the bullies I encountered.

I was teased often and by many kids during grammar school and junior high. When I started high school, many of my classmates had gone off to different schools. I was in a new setting with new people and I made friends with many upperclassmen and the bullying pretty much subsided. However, I still can feel that knot I'd get in my stomach before I'd head out the door to go walk to kindergarten, knowing that I'd be taunted and tormented all the way there.

No kid should have to go through that and I was happy to learn about this No-Naming Calling Week and other efforts that are being made to stop bullying in schools. A few clicks of the mouse and I found a lot of information on proposed legislation on bullying, tips for staff and parents on combating bullying, signs to look for to tell if your child is a bully or a victim, statistics and outcomes of bullying. I truly hope area schools will embrace this idea for No-Naming Calling Week and will take steps to inform students about the consequences of bullying.

I also recalled an episode of the Dr. Phil show that was on bullying and checked the Web site, www.drphil.com. By typing the word "bullying" in the search field, I found information on that show, in which his son, Jay, visited a middle school in Texas to educate the students and staff on bullying and how to stop it. He offered an "Anti-Bullying Pledge," which was a document signed by individual students, teachers and parents as a vow not to bully and to do their part to prevent and stop bullying. It indicated that even if you are not a bully, you bear some responsibility if you see it happening and do nothing to stop it. That document is available on the Web site and would be a great tool to use during No Name-Calling Week.

Eliminating bullying is something that I think every school should strive for and I hope this information will encourage a teacher, administrator, parent or student to initiate activities for No Name-Calling Week. If anyone locally is participating in this event or would like to know about other Web sites that offered information on the topic, I'd like to hear from you.

Kids have the right idea about making friends

April 3, 2004

We parents are the ones who are supposed to do the teaching, right? Well that's generally true, but there are so many things we learn from our kids as well.

Sometimes in watching our children, we are reminded of our flaws when they are reflected back at us. Sometimes they teach us about how precious it is to be naive. Other times they teach us that simplicity is the answer to things that become overcomplicated in our adult world.

During a trip to the park last week with my boys on a warm, breezy day, I was reminded of how easily children can make friends as I observed my kids playing, particularly my soon-to-be five-year-old. If kids that age see something fun going on, they just jump in, completely unconcerned with the possibility of rejection or the fear of dismissal.

Not every kid jumps right in. There are many shy kids out there, but at this age children are also not afraid to go up to other kids and invite them to play along. If you're shy, it's probably easier to be included when you're four than when you are 40.

From watching my own children and kids of friends, as well as my experience of being four years old myself long ago, I've noticed how quick most kids are to mingle with one another, whether it is a best friend or just another child they encounter at the grocery store or at the park. They can be completely uninhibited without provocation or concern for consequences, something adults can usually achieve only with the use of alcohol or drugs. The older we get, often the more nervous we become about interacting with others on an individual basis and in groups.

As we arrived at the park, I sat on a bench with the baby and the other three went up the stairs of the playground equipment. Soon they were running wildly, chasing each other around. My four-year-old passed another child who was standing back and watching. "Come on kid," he said, motioning for the child to follow. Within 30 seconds, the child was right alongside my son and another little girl had joined in. The three were soon playing hide and seek together.

Then when my son noticed a little boy admiring the motorized jeep his brothers had driven to the park, he invited him in for a ride. He then asked the other boy if he wanted to drive. It was adorable to watch him with the stranger riding around and laughing as if they were old friends.

Once we got back to the house, he played with the great-grandson of my neighbor who was visiting and is the same age. The two bonded quickly and went on a mission with my older son to find clues and solve a mystery.

What I observed got me thinking about how wonderful it is that kids can interact like that. If there was a group of grown men who were playing baseball at the park, how likely would it be that another man who was alone would ask if he could join in? Or if a guy walked into a bar alone and saw a couple guys sitting at a table having a good time, what are the chances that he would go over and ask to be part of the group?

How often does it happen that a woman is in a store and sees someone else shopping and says, "Want to go over to cosmetics with me for a makeover" or "Hey, want me to push you in the cart?"

Such antics are acceptable when you're in kindergarten, but don't go over as well in the grown-up world.

If an adult outsider politely asked to join in with a group in a bar, a baseball field or at the mall, he or she may be obliged—after hesitation—but likely the group would be skeptical or judgmental.

Maybe they'd be accepting of the individual initially, until he was gone and then they'd talk about him negatively. It's too bad that in such a situation we can't just all shrink back down and play hide and seek together at the park and remember how easy it should be.

Everyone needs a friend like Fran

March 12, 2004

Last weekend I attended the wedding of an adorable young couple. I guess I've known the groom for about 10 years, and I just met the bride a couple of years ago. However I wasn't really there as a guest of the groom or bride. I was invited to share the special day with one of my best friends. She wasn't a bridesmaid or a sister of the bride. Not even the mother of the bride or groom. My good friend is a woman of 70, named Fran, the grandmother of the groom.

I had a wonderful time at the reception. Everyone including Fran, looked stunning. It was a good party. And, yes, Fran was out there partying with the best of them. She was on the dance floor more than many of the people half her age.

I first met Fran when I was 16 years old and working as a student aide in the district office of my high school. She's someone who leaves quite an impression on you. She's someone who tells it like it is. She doesn't beat around the bush. She's not about to get stepped on or pushed around. If she doesn't like something, you can expect to hear about it. She can be a little rough sometimes, but in an endearing sort of way. Even when she gets under your skin, you secretly wish you had the guts to do what she does. She's definitely one of a kind.

At first, some people aren't sure how to take her. Either they love her for her honesty or are completely offended. I remember one secretary that she worked with telling me that after her first phone conversation with Fran, about thirty years ago, she hung up the phone and said, "That's the rudest person I've ever talked to." Eventually, Fran grew on her and they had a good working relationship.

Fran had a good working relationship with most of the people she worked with, especially some of her bosses. She wasn't intimidated by them and they had a mutual respect for one another. She kept that office running like a well-oiled machine. She could simultaneously type a memo, make coffee for a meeting and get a board packet out with her eyes closed. She had a system for everything she did and she did it with lightening speed.

Fran also has a sense of humor and that's what some of her bosses and other co-workers always liked best about her. I remember one assistant principal, who was like her in some ways, especially when it came to language—they both swore like sailors. The two would antagonize each other like brother and sister. They were always going at it. Neither would let up. He's one person who really gave her a run for her money.

Fran has not had an easy life and I think that's what has made her the way she is: a tough exterior with a heart of gold. She went through a lot—lost her mother at an early age, raised a disabled son as a single parent and lost him as a teenager, overcame serious health problems. Her unfortunate circumstances hardened her over the years, but those who know her well know what a caring and extraordinary person she is.

What else can I say about dear Frances? She's persistent. If she wants something, she's not satisfied until she gets it.

When she's right she's right. You don't want to pick a fight with her or argue with her. You'll never win.

She's generous. Whether it's buying a new car for her granddaughter or donating the bingo money she's won to the St. Jude Children's Hospital, she's done a lot for others.

She's sentimental. Even though she comes off as being tough, I've seen her eyes tear up many times when she's talking about something close to her heart.

MOM MOMENTS

She'll kill me for writing this—but she's got a bad habit of accumulating items that appear on infomercials. She doesn't know what she'll do with it, but she's got to have it. I can't tell you how many silly gadgets she's bought that she has no intention of ever using.

She's got willpower. This time of year she agonizes over cheesecake she can't eat, because she successfully gives up sweets each year for lent.

She's the most energetic 70-year-old you'll ever meet. She's always on the go—water aerobics, bingo, movies, dinner—and she's planning on taking up country line dancing again. That's something the two of us enjoyed together years ago.

She's also got a schoolgirl crush on her favorite singer, George Strait. She never misses a concert when he's in the area. She's got every album of his. When she retired, we presented her with all kinds of George Strait memorabilia. Some co-workers took a photo of him and pasted her picture beside him. That picture even went on the cake!

Fran once told me, "People may not like me, but they'll damn sure never forget me." I don't think she ever realized how many people have appreciated her character. I'd be willing to say that there are very few who don't like her. But she's got the second part right. Anyone who has ever met her can surely say she's unforgettable.

Everyone needs good 'old' friends

July 13, 2004

I don't know why, but for some reason I've always related better to people older than me. As a freshman in high school, I often hung out with an older crowd of seniors, which was how I met my husband.

Once I began working after high school, many of my co-workers were much older, but I always got along well with them. In fact, for most of my working years, my best friends were women who were old enough to be my mother, or even my grandmother.

When I got married and we moved into our house, my next-door neighbor was a sweet lady who was old enough to by my grandmother, but whom I adored and spent a lot of time with. We also got to be friends with another neighbor, a man in his 80's, who inspired my son to start his own vegetable garden.

And as a young child, my best friend was the grandchild of a couple who lived next door to my parents. While that friend has married and moved out of state, I keep in touch with her grandparents and invite them to all our family parties.

Maybe I'm drawn to older people because I never had grandparents. None that I really knew, anyway. One grandfather died before I was born. The other died when I was a toddler. His wife died not long after that. And my father's mother, who died when I was around 8 or

9, spent her last years living in Minneapolis and I didn't really get to know her.

I always longed for grandparents who would coddle me and spoil me and give me their undivided attention. I would spend time at friends' houses around their grandparents and it always seemed like older people were less critical and more affectionate to children.

Anyway, I'm still good friends with many of those ladies I worked with who are many years older than I am. We get together occasionally for lunch or dinner or parties or call each other to chat.

Two of them are mothers of one son and I think each of them appreciated our relationship, having never had a daughter. One of them, Jeanette, hemmed my prom dress and got me some sparkling earrings and a necklace to wear with it that I still cherish.

The other, June, visited me in the hospital when I had my first son. Since only parents and grandparents were allowed to visit in the Neo-Natal ICU, we told a little white lie and made her "grandma" so that she could come in to see her "grandson." She also visited when my second son was admitted to the hospital at 6 days old, bringing me breakfast and letting me cry on her shoulder. I won't reveal her age, but June is celebrating a significant birthday this month and I was honored to be invited to celebrate the event with her family at a recent party.

Both talented ladies knitted baby blankets for me that I plan to pass down as my children have children.

Another I worked closely with, Jeanine, was a very sweet and funny lady. I felt like part of her family. I always knew what was going on with her kids and friends. She's someone that would do anything you'd ask her to do. I remember during my first pregnancy telling her I had a craving for oranges, but that I never ate them because I hated to peel them. She started bringing oranges to work and would peel them for me.

Another good friend, Mary Ann, worked side by side with me for years and I got to know all about her family, too. And Fran, who I've written about in this column before, is one of a kind. I've attended family weddings of both this past year and enjoy seeing their families grow with the addition of grandchildren (or great grandchildren). Maybe it's their experience and wisdom that I'm drawn to. For some it's their humorous or outrageous personalities. Whatever the reason, I love each one of them and am thankful to have such good 'old' friends.

Nothing can beat that first car

August 6, 2004

I've had many conversations with people about old cars and about their first car. No matter how old you get, your first car is something that you never seem to forget. If you close your eyes you can see it right in front of you and can imagine yourself sitting behind the wheel again. You remember what you paid for it, how you felt when you first drove it and what songs you'd hear coming from the radio or the 8-track player.

I started dating my husband when I was in high school. He was always working on cars with his buddy. They'd pick up a lot of the cars they had for a few hundred dollars, race them around and abuse them until they died before junking them. Looking back now, I could kick myself for letting him let go of many of them. There was the 1977 Chevelle, the two 1976 Chrysler New Yorkers, the 1971 Oldsmobile Cutlass, the 1970 Chevy Nova and the 1968 Buick Skylark.

My first car was one that he bought for me for $500, a light yellow 1977 Chevy Monte Carlo. He always insisted that these big old "boats" were the safest thing to drive and balked at the thought of me getting a little Yugo or Chevette. I certainly did feel like I was driving a boat, but I adapted to it quickly. I think the cars we used in driver education class were Chevy Corsicas, so there was a significant size difference between the two.

I drove that car for about a year and then I splurged on a maroon-colored 1980 Chevy Caprice for $2,300. The car wasn't quite as large as the Monte Carlo, so it seemed easy to drive in comparison. However, it was far from being a compact car.

When I got the car in 1989, I think it had around 60,000 miles on it, but it had obviously been well taken care of. It had power windows, doors, seats and trunk and a plush maroon interior. I was in heaven. I can't tell you how much I miss that car. I drove it until 1996 when my son was two-years-old and I leased a Nissan mini-van. Now I drive a full-size Chevy conversion van, so I've graduated from driving "boats" to driving "buses."

My husband, who spent much of his school career in shop class, taught me a lot about cars when we first met. We'd go to shows and admire antique cars or we'd hang out at his buddy's garage where they'd work on one of his friend's old GTO's.

For a time I was really into it. I would leisurely flip through a Chilton's manual or a car guide. I could glance at a car as it passed down the road and identify the make and model, usually getting within a year or two of its year.

Cars aren't like that anymore. They aren't distinct. They don't come in those unusual metallic brown shades or pastels like mint green or sky blue or the very unattractive olive green hues. You seldom see a car with wood paneling on the doors anymore, unless it's a PT Cruiser.

Sure, vehicles today may be more comfortable, with contoured, heated seats. They may be smarter, with more gauges and buttons and electronic switches. The sound system may be better. They may have more safety features. They get better gas mileage. They may even come with a television and DVD player.

Even so, none of them compares to that 1977 Monte Carlo.

Events of 9/11 still haunting to this day

September 11, 2004

Each generation has a tragic event to call its own.

For you, it may have been the bombing of Pearl Harbor or the assassination of President Kennedy.

The first tragedy that I recall well was the explosion of the Space Shuttle Challenger in 1986. I was in Mr. Prno's eighth-grade language arts class at Lincoln School in Dolton. My stomach was grumbling because it was close to lunchtime. There was a knock on the door. Mr. Prno went out into the hall for a couple minutes and returned with a somber look, telling us about the explosion and telling us to bow our head for a moment of silence.

Three years ago today, I was eight months pregnant with my third child. I woke up not feeling well and called work to say that I wouldn't be in that day. I went back to sleep for a while and then got in the shower. As I was in there, my husband stuck his head in the door and said that my sister had called and told him to turn on the television because a tower at the World Trade Center had been hit by a plane.

By the time I got out of the shower, the second tower had been hit.

"Do you realize how many people are in there?" my husband asked.

Soon after, he called to me in the other room to tell me that one of the towers had collapsed.

In one of the days following the attacks, I remember everyone in the office gathering in the conference room, joining hands and listening to a co-worker say a prayer. There were people in the room of several different religions, some who faithfully attended church each Sunday and some who probably hadn't set foot in a church in months or even years, but they were all there.

I'm sure most people can remember the circumstances of that time very well. For those who were in the vicinity that day and for those who lost loved ones, I'm sure its something that haunts them on a daily basis.

While some time has gone by, it's something that will never go away and that will never escape our memories.

Eating habits of the young are puzzling

October 9, 2004

I know I'm not the only parent who wonders why kids eat the way they do. I guess rule number one is kids want to eat what tastes good, which is usually junk food.

So then why is it that some kids welcome vegetables while others turn their noses up to anything green? Vegetables taste good to some kids, but others would rather eat dirt.

One theory is kids follow their parents' lead. That sounds reasonable, but you've got parents who eat tofu and their children won't touch it. I've also heard that kids need to be exposed to many different foods, but just because you plant a plate of sushi in front of them doesn't mean they'll be willing to give it a try.

Some kids are just naturally picky and trying new foods is just not for them. Other kids are more adventurous and don't mind trying calamari or artichokes just to see what they're like.

Of my four kids, I've got two that will eat almost anything, and I've got two who will eat almost nothing. They've all been raised in the same house. They've had the same parental examples. They've been exposed to the same foods. I know some child-care experts will suggest that it's not about food, but rather control or other issues. I'm not going to go there. I just wonder how kids' tastes can vary so much.

My oldest son is quite unusual when it comes to his diet. If you gave him a choice between a salmon, steak and a cheeseburger, he'd take the salmon. If you offered him baked orange roughy or a cookie, again, he'd likely choose the fish. Actually, I haven't found a seafood he doesn't like. When we order pizza, he wants anchovies on it. He'd rather dip shrimp in cocktail sauce than potato chips in dip. He even requested clams one time when we were shopping at the seafood counter, so I bought some, boiled them and he ate every one. He also enjoys canned sardines and smoked herring when he visits his grandfather. When he asked me to make him a pickled herring sandwich for lunch, I said "no" for two reasons. The first is that I don't like the smell. The second is that I don't think he'd be real popular at school when the whole cafeteria smelled like fish.

He also loves to have a salad with light dressing, a bowl of spinach or a serving of asparagus and he'll try almost anything.

My 5-year-old could eat better, but could eat worse. He does like broccoli, carrots, potatoes and peas, but he'd abandon them all in a second for an ice cream cone.

The foods that my almost-3-year-old eats can be counted on my two hands. He'll eat macaroni and cheese, chicken nuggets, hot dogs, yogurt, apples, peanut butter sandwiches, chips, cereal, an occasional raw carrot and anything with sugar in it. And he's stubborn even if he's hungry. He'd rather starve than eat something that's not on that list.

My 1-year-old only has refused one food—cheese. Anything else that's put on his highchair tray is inhaled. So far so good. Hopefully, it will stay that way.

This is the first column to appear as a "Mom Moments" article

SOMETIMES CAREGIVERS NEED A HELPING HAND

October 16, 2005

I figured I should start this column with a little introduction. Some of you may have seen my byline before. I've been a Times correspondent for the past five years and previously wrote a column for the local Illinois section. In my past columns, I wrote about many things, but often about my life as a mom to a house full of boys, who are now ages 11, 6, 4, 2 and 6 months. Any writer who also is a parent will tell you that children provide you with plenty of material. So, in this column, I'll share some of those memorable moments that make you laugh and cry and sigh and thank your lucky stars that these little people are in your lives.

Now that I've got that out of the way, I'll explain my most recent parenting dilemma. As a mom, I often find that six, seven, maybe eight arms would come in handy. However, these days I'm down to one.

On a Sunday evening, when my 6-year-old returned from a long day with grandpa, he was too zonked out to get up and head for his bed. So, I figured I'd pick him up and carry him there. Well, 42 pounds in your arms and a flight of stairs don't mix well. Down we went. Mom broke his fall and her arm.

Needless to say, caring for children with one arm isn't easy. I'm always multitasking and using both hands for different functions. I've learned to do many things with one hand over the years, but there are certain things you just can't. Ever tried changing a dirty diaper on a squirming 6-month-old one handed? It's not easy. Ever drained the grease from a pan of ground beef without two hands? It can't be done.

So, I've found myself on unfamiliar (and somewhat uncomfortable) ground. I've had to ask for help and depend on others. Maybe it's a female thing, maybe it's a mom thing or maybe it's just me, but I have a hard time accepting assistance from other people because I feel this overwhelming pressure to reciprocate. I'm sure a lot of people can relate.

The past couple of weeks, I've just had to abandon that little mental running list of repayment and had to accept that there are things I'm just not able to do. That means taking people up on their offers of help and reaching out and asking others to do some of the things I can't. It's times like this that you truly realize how many friends you have and how handy it would be to have a few extra arms.

Halloween: The second best holiday of the year

October 30, 2005

I recall a Christmas special that would air each year in which the characters sang about the "most wonderful time of the year." Coming in a close second would be Halloween, in my opinion.

Speaking from my experience of once being a little kid, Halloween is a pretty big deal. There aren't many kids out there who don't have a good time dressing up and collecting free candy.

If you're a grown-up (or a big kid), it may be a big deal to you, too. I know it is to me. There are no other days during the year when you're able to dress as a princess or a ninja without someone questioning your sanity. It's also a day when you get to see people in your neighborhood that often slip in and out of their homes without you even realizing they are there. It's a time when people acknowledge each other and there's just this joyful atmosphere, especially when we get one of the 75-degree days for trick-or-treating.

The Halloween season is a lot of fun for me since I have young children. I love to see how excited they get about their costumes and how the most pressing difficulty in their life is trying to decide what to be. I've got one who started out wanting to be the Hulk, then Batman, then Spider-Man, then a firefighter, then Spider-Man, then a Power Ranger. We bought the Spider-Man costume weeks ago, but since we've got all the others from past Halloweens, he's been changing his mind quite often. I'm still waiting for the final verdict since there still are a few hours left for him to ponder his decision.

Halloween also was a lot of fun for me when I was younger. I recall the competition between my sisters and me over who would collect the most candy. I remember one year setting out in the dark alone after my sisters had given up, just so I could add a few more pieces to my bag. When we got home, we spread all our candy out on the floor and counted each piece, then went through our annual negotiations of "I'll trade you a pack of Skittles, two Tootsie Rolls and a piece of gum for that Snickers bar." The awful peanut butter kisses and Bit O' Honeys went into a pile for my dad.

My favorite Halloween was the year that I was 10 years old. I somehow talked my mom into letting me have a Halloween party. With our playhouse transformed into a haunted house and a backyard bonfire for roasting hot dogs and marshmallows, I entertained a yard full of kids in costume. I was a bride, recycling the bouquet that I'd caught just a couple weeks earlier at my brother's wedding.

So, this year, whether you're an active participant, a bystander witnessing your little one enjoy the season or just the person handing out the candy, I hope you, too, enjoy the season. May it bring you a few treats and a lot of smiles.

Appreciation is important lesson for kids

November 13, 2005

As parents, there are values that we try to instill in our children. They don't always stick, but we try. Each parent has a different approach. While there are many ideals that we'd like our children to follow, each parent emphasizes different values that they'd like their child to adopt.

One important lesson that I've tried to teach my children is to appreciate those who do things for you, whether it's being grateful to a stranger who holds a door open for you or expressing thanks to a friend who gives you a birthday gift.

I also let them know that there are many people who do things for them that they don't ever see or meet that deserve our gratitude. I try to get across the fact that there are people who serve in the military to protect the way we live and to allow us to have the freedoms we have. It likely goes in one ear and out the other when you're telling a 3-year-old, but eventually it sinks in.

While it's something I try to get across throughout the year, there are certain times when you think about it a little more. This time of year, as Veteran's Day is observed, is one of them.

Lately, through a PTA project and some articles I've been writing, I've been in touch with some veterans, some current military personnel and some family members of individuals who are currently deployed.

I know that the little bits and pieces of what I hear are just a fraction of what those in the military have to face. And hearing it described is far from being there. It can't allow you to feel what they've felt, but it makes you more aware. That awareness spills into your everyday life.

As you adjust the thermostat to make you comfortable, you think of the soldiers bearing temperatures of 115 degrees on a daily basis. As you sit down to eat dinner or reach for something sweet to finish off your meal, you wonder what our servicemen and servicewomen are eating and how long it's been since they've had a good home-cooked meal or a piece of homemade apple pie.

The more aware you are of their circumstances, the more you can appreciate their sacrifices. Each holiday there is something new to tell my kids about—another person, a different situation, a new place.

If feels good to see what happens when a lesson like this one does sink in.

My oldest, now 11, always makes signs to put around the house, pulls out American flags and plays patriotic music when Memorial Day, Independence Day, Patriot Day and Veterans Day roll around. Sometimes he decorates his bike and motorized toys and has his own parade around the block to honor our nation's heroes or sets up chairs and does a service for whoever will watch. He puts together care packages to send overseas. He asks about relatives who have served in the military and writes biographies about them.

He takes time to think of them and appreciate them and as a parent, it's nice to see that one of your lessons has been taken to heart.

Children cherish one on one time with parents

November 27, 2005

No matter what age a child is, he or she enjoys spending one-on-one time with Mom or Dad. For most kids, that special time is something that is cherished. Memories are made on outings, fishing trips and shopping dates that stick in a child's mind for years.

I always enjoyed the time I was able to spend with my mom or my dad when it was just the two of us. Growing up with five siblings, including twin sisters born just over two years after me, life in our house was often chaotic and my sisters and I competed for our parent's attention.

It was always a treat when just my dad and I would make a trip to the grocery store. We'd wander down the aisles looking for bargains or for Dad's favorite snacks and we'd usually share a Mr. Goodbar in the car on the way home. Things were quiet and we had time to chat.

The same trip to the store with my younger sisters along would have started with a fight over who was sitting in the front seat, followed by a fight over who was sitting in the cart or pushing the cart, followed by arguments over which cereal to buy. That was on a good day. Sometimes there was chasing, hair pulling and a clean up in aisle nine.

My dad worked a second job for many years to pay the bills. For a few years, he was a deliveryman for a small, family-owned pizza place on weekends. I remember looking forward to Saturday nights when I'd get to go along with him. When you're five-years-old, it doesn't get any better than a night with your favorite food and your favorite guy.

Since I remember how special those one-one-times were, I make sure that I fit in some one-on-one time with each of the kids. Each time we've added a child to our family, it's gotten a little harder. Sometimes it happens several times a week. Sometimes it's a struggle to get in a few precious moments alone.

Sometimes I'm lucky enough to sneak off to the movies with one of them or I get a chance to take them out to eat. Other times it's a simple trip to the store or a ride to the bank. Maybe it's a few minutes to read a book just to one of them or a few quiet moments on my lap in the rocking chair.

Life is hectic and sometimes it takes a little nudge, like last week when my six-year-old requested stopping at Burger King after school for a treat. "Can't we go, Mom, just you and me?" he asked.

I still enjoy spending time alone with my dad, although it doesn't happen much anymore. Recently, he called to invite me to a show with him. My mom wasn't feeling well and my brother had bought tickets to see Bob Newhart as an anniversary present for them. I jumped at the chance and had a great time. I may not be five-years-old anymore, but I still cherish one-on-one time with my dad.

Traditions keep the holidays merry

December 11, 2005

'Tis the season for snow and shopping, candy canes and wreaths, reindeer and Santa and lots of holiday traditions, from kissing under the mistletoe to making fudge to viewing classic holiday movies.

I love traditions. When my first son was born I was intent on carrying on holiday traditions from my childhood and starting some of my own. These special routines that you could count on year after year were always a big part of what made the season so merry.

One holiday tradition that both my husband and I enjoyed as children was decorating a real Christmas tree. My mom always loved the smell of a real tree and to her it was well worth the mess of falling needles to have the scent of fresh evergreen fill the house.

Decorating for Christmas in our house entailed a long ordeal of my dad putting the tree in the stand and shifting it a little to the left and noticing it was crooked. He'd then shift it a little to the right and it would be just a little off again. We'd go around and around until everyone could agree that it was straight.

Then came the ritual of unpacking the ornaments and reminiscing about where each one came from. My mom had special ornaments that had to be placed in a certain spot so that they were visible from her favorite chair.

My sisters and I would make popcorn in the hot-air popper (microwaves were not yet common kitchen appliances at that time).

We'd pull needles and thread out of Mom's sewing kit and make popcorn garland that we'd carefully place on the tree.

Each year we'd make ornaments with my dad, gluing foam balls onto sugar cones. Then we'd make snowflakes from tissue paper that would hang from the ceiling around the tree.

Getting a real tree has become a tradition that my husband and I have carried on with our own kids. Ever since I met my husband eighteen years ago, we'd take a ride with his parents to buy a tree from a Wisconsin farmer who'd haul his trees down to Alsip. He later moved into a lot a little farther, but we kept going back. We finally got to the point where my in-laws had to drive a separate car and we pulled a trailer (for the three trees we'd purchase) with our full-size van to fit everyone in. Each year, after selecting trees, we'd head over to Grandma and Grandpa's house and have dinner and the kids would play.

One year I thought it would be nice to cut down our own tree, but to make a long story short, it was a complete disaster. The next year we were back to visit Ken and his lot of trees.

This year, we got a note in the mail that Ken wouldn't be at his regular location to sell trees anymore. It made me think of a line my mom used occasionally—"All good things must come to an end."

We ended up finding a place just about five minutes away from home where we bought a decent tree for about half of what we'd been paying Ken. Grandma and Grandpa didn't come along and decided not to get a tree this year. We picked up dinner after getting our tree and went home. The next day we all decorated it together and reminisced over ornaments and wall hangings with tiny handprints. It was a little sad to see our annual tree tradition come to an end, but when one tradition ends, it's usually the beginning of another.

All I want for Christmas is eight hours of sleep

December 25, 2005

It's 11:14 p.m. and I finally decide to head to bed. The boys have been asleep for hours, but I've been folding laundry, checking e-mail, making lunches and paying bills. It's been a long, tiring day and I'm ready for some shuteye.

Nine minutes later, I hear a soft, but constant, cry. I tiptoe to my 8-month-old's crib, feel around for his pacifier (aka binky) and place it back in his mouth. He gets quiet! Yeah!

It lasts 21 minutes. I've just dozed off when I hear another cry. I get up and repeat the routine and settle back into bed. This time it lasts 23 minutes. When I return to his crib, the "stick the binky in his mouth and run" trick doesn't work. He keeps crying.

To avoid disturbing everyone in the house, I bring him into bed where he snuggles and squirms and we both drift off. He sleeps a little, whines a little, eats a little and snoozes some more. At 3:04 a.m., he's quite restless, so we sit in the rocking chair until he nods off and I return him to his crib. I manage to get in almost two hours of sleep before he's up again and back in bed with me. About a half hour later, my 2-year-old is calling for me and it's all over—about 17 or 18 more hours before I'll meet my pillow again.

Sleep deprivation is something I, like most new parents, was totally unprepared for. When I became a mom, I thought that my late nights of partying had prepared me for sleepless nights with a baby.

Not! When you don't have kids and you party until 4 a.m., you can spend the following day in bed making up for it. Not so when you've got little ones.

And just as no two children have the same personality, no two have the same sleep patterns. Of my five children, this one isn't the worst sleeper, believe it or not. And the best sleeper of the bunch slept from 11 p.m. until 4 a.m. the night he came home from the hospital and it just got better from there.

I'll get to the point. I realize that today is Christmas. I'm sure that by now Santa has filled all his requests and is at home with his feet up, sipping a latte and watching reruns of "Seinfeld" or a good documentary on the Discovery Channel. Anyway, it doesn't hurt to try. So, Santa, if you wouldn't mind putting in a good word with your buddy, Mr. Sandman, I sure would appreciate it!

Many memories were made in 2005

January 8, 2006

At the end of each year, I enjoy looking back at the events that happened during that year on the news. I'm always amazed at how short our memories are and how many events are forgotten by year's end.

Every year there are significant events that happen around the world, in our country and in our community. Some stick with us, but most become lost unless they personally affected us.

Many images of 2005 will be ingrained my head when I'm old and gray. There are major things the year will be remembered for. The aftermath of the tsunami, devastation of the southern hurricanes, the continuing War on Terrorism and the White Sox winning the World Series are the events that I'm sure will stand out. Other than that, there are probably not many other headlines that I'll recall. The events that have happened in my own life, within my family, will be much better remembered.

This was the year my oldest son jumped from childhood to adolescence. He became a "preteen" this year. His voice changed. He shot up several inches within a few months. I'll remember watching him on the basketball court and in karate class. I'll remember the waterfall cake we made for his Cub Scout dinner and taking him and his baby brother to a Cubs game.

I'll think about how my 6-year-old started reading books to me this year, how he ran chasing the ball during his soccer games and how much fun he had when his dad spent an afternoon at school making snowmen with his class.

I'll remember how excited my 4-year-old was when he started preschool and when he got his Spider-Man bed. I'll remember his phase of wanting to eat only yogurt for breakfast, lunch and dinner.

I'll think of my 2-year-old and his transition from being the baby to being a big brother. I'll remember how he went from uttering a few words when the year started to babbling sentence after sentence.

Giving birth to my fifth son was the highlight of the year. I'll remember passing my due date and heading to the hospital on April Fool's Day. I'll recall following the condition of the Pope, who passed away the day my son was born. I'll reflect on how rapidly my baby boy changed, crawling and standing with help by the end of the year. I don't think I'll ever forget sitting in a water park with him on vacation singing along to the Beatles song blaring over the speakers as he gave me one of his first big grins.

This was the year that my husband spent five days out of town for school, the longest we've ever been separated. It was the year that a dear uncle died after a long illness. It was the year my sister had her first child (the first girl born in my family in 18 years), my big brother turned the big 50, my niece returned from teaching in Japan for a year and announced her engagement, another niece graduated from high school. There were plenty of personal headlines and they're the ones I'll remember most.

There's a History Lesson in Every Family

January 22, 2006

For generations, storytelling was a big part of family life. Stories were passed on from previous generations in an effort to teach important lessons and see that their heritage would not be forgotten. It's hard for kids today to imagine, but long before iPods, computers and DVD players, family entertainment involved gathering around the dinner table or in front of the fireplace for a family story.

Although family storytelling as a Saturday night event likely doesn't happen very often these days, there still are parents who throw in their two cents now and then, giving a little lesson about how things went on decades ago. My parents often told me stories about their past. They usually started with "In the olden days..." and would continue with recollections of riding around town in rumble seats or of meals that were made from basic cupboard staples to feed a family of eight. They'd mention characters and actors that were foreign to me, like Howdy Doody or Shirley Temple.

The older I get, the more I appreciate all those family stories and find myself reciting them, along with some from my childhood, to my own kids. I also find myself grilling relatives for more information these days, anxious to learn more about what their daily lives were like and some of the obstacles they overcame.

I was amazed during a recent conversation with my dad, who was a payroll clerk during his years in the U.S. Army. More than four decades later, he can rattle off the pay grades of each rank as if he just processed a batch of checks yesterday. During that conversation, my father also explained that his mother, who married in 1921, kept her marriage a secret so that she could continue teaching. Since only unmarried women could be teachers, my grandparents went to a different county to get married and lived separately, so that she could finish out the school year.

A recent visit to the U-505 Submarine exhibit at the Museum of Science and Industry made me aware of some family history I'd never given much thought to. My husband pointed out a large photo to my sons of some German toddlers sitting on a curb with a bombed-out building behind them.

"This is what it was like when your grandpa was little," he told them. "You guys don't realize how lucky you are."

I knew my father-in-law immigrated to the U.S. in his late teens, but never thought about how scary, difficult and uncertain his childhood must have been as World War II began in Europe when he was just a baby being raised in Berlin. He's never talked much about his childhood. I guess I can understand why.

In every family, there's a lot to learn if you ask, look and really listen. And just when you think you've heard it all, something new comes up. So, even if I bore the pants off my little guys, I'll continue to re-tell stories and prod for more.

BE KIND TO THOSE IN OUR CHILDREN'S LIVES

February 18, 2006

In our crazy, fast paced world it's easy to get wrapped up in ourselves and our own needs. Even the nicest of people have days where things are harried and they aren't quite themselves and do something out of character. We've all had moments where we haven't been likeable. Today is our day to make amends. Today is the final day of Random Acts of Kindness week. Haven't heard of it? You can go to actsofkindness.org to learn more about the Random Acts of Kindness Foundation which, according to the mission statement on their website "inspires people to practice kindness and to 'pass it on' to others."

The idea behind Random Acts of Kindness week is to encourage generosity among people of all kinds towards other people of all kinds. The website offers ideas for projects, but there are no rules. The title is self-explanatory. The acts of kindness are random—they should be spontaneous, casual, unplanned, indiscriminate, without expectation of reciprocation. They can be done for a family member, a friend, an acquaintance or a stranger. They can involve a large commitment of time or money. They can be as small as holding the door open for a stranger or offering a smile and a friendly "hello."

Sure, we all have good intentions at some point during the year. This is the time to put them into action. This is also a chance to expose our children to charity, to volunteering and to finding ways to lend a hand to those less fortunate. Bring up the idea to your children and I'm sure they'll come up with many thoughtful acts.

This is also a good opportunity to express appreciation to those who make a difference in our children's lives, but to whom we don't express our thanks often enough. Even though today is the final day of Random Acts of Kindness Week, the thoughts will mean just as much tomorrow or later this week.

So, take a few minutes to do something random and kind in the coming days for those who are important in your children's lives (and maybe those you overlooked on Valentine's Day.) Send a note of thanks to your child's teacher or visit the class for a few hours to help out. Buy lunch for the janitor who sweeps up the floors at school each day. Give some flowers to the crossing guard who watches over them. Bake a plate of cookies for the school secretary. Give your babysitter a tip. Invite Grandma over for dinner. Treat the bus driver to a cup of coffee. Thank your spouse for all that he or she does. Jump in and give the coach a few minutes to relax on the bench. Buy a new book from the school librarian's wish list or volunteer to help with a project. Give the school principal a high five for his hard work and buy him a roll of Tums just for laughs. The possibilities are endless. Once you're on a roll, you'll find how easy it is to be kind and how good your acts will make you feel.

Hats off to local mom who's following her dream

March 19, 2006

I had a column prepared to turn in for today, but then I tuned into "Nashville Star" on Tuesday night and I decided to switch topics. Most readers probably know that one of the finalists on the show is a Schererville resident, Nicole Jamrose.

Even if you're not a fan of country music or of the show, there has been plenty of buzz in the area about Jamrose and her trip to Nashville to appear on the show after being selected from about 20,000 people who auditioned. You'd have to be living under a rock not to have heard about it.

I first heard about Jamrose after reading an article about her in The Times a few weeks ago. I tuned in to the show's season premiere Tuesday with hopes that she'd make the region proud, but was hesitant to expect too much, only to be disappointed.

I don't mean that as an insult to Jamrose. I just figured that a girl from Schererville, going up against many real Southerners might not quite fit in. I was very wrong. She proved that you don't have to come from the Tennessee foothills, the Alabama countryside or a Texas cattle ranch to be able to belt out a rockin' country song.

Even if she hadn't been from Northwest Indiana, I'm sure she'd be the one I'd be rooting for because she's the mom of two little ones. From what I recall seeing at the start of the show as each finalist was introduced, Jamrose is the oldest one of the bunch and the only parent. It would be great to see her win the competition for many reasons.

Obviously, because she's from the area, I'd like to see her win. Secondly, with her being older than the rest of the group, I would think this might be her last attempt at seriously pursuing a big-time career in country music. She mentioned on the show that she'd spent years trying to get into the business after college and then settled down, got married and had children.

If she were not to win the competition, I don't think it would be likely that she'd pack up her husband and kids and move to Nashville to keep trying. Maybe I'm wrong. I don't know her, but I know there are a lot of young singers on the show who have plenty of time and talent to continue pursuing this dream. Seems to me that Jamrose has paid her dues. And I think her experience showed in her performance.

I'd also like to see her win because I do think she's one of the best singers and performers in the group, although she does have some tough competition. In my opinion, she's the best by far of the females, however, I think the guys will be tough to beat.

Most of all, I'd like to see Jamrose succeed because she'd be a big inspiration to all the other moms out there who have put their dreams on the back burner when their children arrived. I know there are many talented mothers in the region who have what it takes to achieve their dreams, whether it's opening a restaurant, seeing their artwork hang in a gallery, writing a book or recording a country music album. Jamrose just might remind them not to give up on those dreams.

Let's all hope that when she comes back to Northwest Indiana it will be as a "Nashville Star." Either way, she's the only gal on the show who will be lucky enough to get to go home and sing to her two littlest fans every day.

Where were you a year ago?

April 6, 2006

Do you remember what you were doing exactly one year ago? Most people might have a hard time remembering details of something that happened a half-year ago, a month ago or possibly even a week ago. It's pretty difficult to try and recall what you were doing exactly 365 days ago. Except for a handful of memorable events, like weddings or birthdays, or significant world events, most of the other days just blur together when we try to recall them a year later.

What happened on this day is something people likely will remember because it was the date of a significant world event, the death of Pope John Paul II. When important figures die, people often can recall where they were and what they were doing the moment they heard the news. I'm sure if I asked a handful of people if they remember what they were doing when John Kennedy or Martin Luther King Jr. were shot, they could tell me. Other people might remember hearing news of the death of Elvis or John Lennon. Some people may recall where they were when Princess Diana died.

I wasn't born yet when John Kennedy died, but I remember when his wife, Jacqueline Kennedy, died on May 19, 1994. The reason that I remember that event nearly 12 years later is because my eldest son was born that day. I recall turning on the television that evening in my postpartum room and watching coverage about her death and clips about her life.

April 2, 2005, is a day that will stay in my memory because it was not only the day of Pope John Paul II's death, but the birth of my youngest son. I arrived at the hospital around 10:30 p.m. April 1 and recall hospital staff talking about the pope's condition as I was settling into my room. After my son was born about four hours later, I remember turning on the television to continuing coverage from Rome.

So many details of that day are still fresh in my mind. I remember the moment he entered this world and looking into his eyes for the first time.

I recall walking to the nursery a few hours after he was born and looking into the nursery to find wall-to-wall bassinets with pink blankets. My little guy was the only newborn wrapped in blue when I peeked in on him.

I remember being visited by my twin sisters later in the day. They greeted me with a blue stuffed bear that my 5-year-old named Snuggly Wuggly Buggly, a balloon and a handful of candy bars I'd been looking forward to after following a diabetic diet for my third trimester. My husband visited soon after with my other sons who were all very excited to meet their new brother and two of the baby's grandparents and my brother and sister-in-law also made it there that day.

I recall my sweet roommate during my stay. I can't recall her first name, but her last name was Carey, so our phone calls kept getting sent to the wrong phone lines. She was a beautiful African-American woman in her late 20s.

I was intrigued by her accent and when I answered my phone to get a call intended for her and heard someone speaking French, I had to find out a little more about where she was from. The call had been from her sister. She explained she had grown up in Liberia, but came to the U.S. during Liberia's civil war. Her parents were killed during the war. She was separated from her siblings and she had to leave her daughter behind.

Once she got to the U.S., she worked at Wal-Mart and sent money to her uncle to help find her siblings who were believed to be in refugee camps. She later found out that her uncle had kept the money and built himself a nice house.

MOM MOMENTS

Being naive to Liberia's culture, I asked her if it was anything like what was depicted on my favorite show, "ER." She laughed. She said one of her in-laws actually asked her if she lived in a tree, but in reality she lived in a large home. I believe she described it as having five bedrooms and five bathrooms. I knew very little about Liberia, but doubted that most families resided in five-bedroom homes.

"What did your father do?" I asked. "Were you from a royal family?" She answered with hesitation that she was. "But I couldn't go back there now. I'd be killed because of it."

She expressed surprise at how little Americans know about the war in her country and that part of the world, in general. She told me to look on the Internet if I wanted to find out more about it and I did.

She was such an interesting person with such a wonderful outlook on life despite all that she'd been through. We had fun chatting and watching television late at night when we were up with our babies.

I'm sure as the years pass, many of the little details of that day will slip from my mind. But right now as I recall what I was doing last year, it's still all very fresh. It was a day that a great man left the earth and the day a great new person entered it.

Siblings play a special role in our lives

April 16, 2006

I had noticed in a magazine article recently that April 10 was National Sibling Day. At first I suspected it was another day created by greeting card companies, but after a little searching on the Internet, I leaned that the day was initiated in 1997 by Claudia Evert, a woman who had lost both her siblings in accidents. She wanted it to be a day when people remembered siblings who had been lost and celebrated the siblings had. The article mentioned that siblings are lifelong friends who know you from cradle to grave. There's no other relationship like that.

I'm sure most people have probably never heard of National Sibling Day. However, I think it's a great idea to set aside a day when we can express our admiration and appreciation for our brothers and sisters. I know I don't let my siblings know often enough how much I love them and how blessed I feel to have them in my life.

I happen to be from a family of six children. I fall in the middle. However, my older siblings are quite a bit older—17, 15 and 14 years older. I also have a set of twin sisters who are two years younger than I am.

It's funny how in families, although they are raised by the same set of parents in the same home, each child is such an individual.

MOM MOMENTS

My oldest brother, Mark, has always been the family comedian. As the oldest, he's always looked out for us. I always enjoyed spending time with him and with his daughters who are now all grown up. Because we live just a few houses apart, he's developed a special relationship with my boys. He often drops in with candy, doughnuts, pizza or other treats and offers them a dollar if they respond correctly to the question, "Who's your favorite uncle?" He's a gem as a brother and an uncle.

My brother, Mike, lives a little further, so I don't get to see him and his wife and son as often. I'm extremely proud of him and his career choice to be a middle school guidance counselor and I've always admired his athletic skills. You know you can go to him for advice and he's happy to help.

My big sister Pam has always been an inspiration to me. When I was younger I wanted nothing more than to be a career woman working on the 26th floor of a downtown office building like her. When we became moms of sons a year apart, it was nice to be going through it along with her. She's one of the most genuine, caring people on the face of the earth.

My little sisters, Becky and Jenny are twins, but couldn't be more different. They're fraternal and look nothing alike. Both are sweet and generous and intelligent and would do anything for you. This summer Jenny will deliver her second daughter and after always living in the area, she moved about 160 miles away. She adores my boys and has always spoiled them. We still talk often, but I really miss having her close by, especially now that she's a mom, too.

Next weekend Becky will be getting married and it will be neat to see her starting a family of her own, also. She's everything I'm not—neat and orderly, a whiz at math and science, a computer geek, into science fiction. Even with all our differences, that sisterly bond exists.

Many people think I'm crazy when they learn that I have five sons. However, after growing up with five wonderful siblings, that's the way I always wanted it. I wanted a houseful of kids who could play with each other, depend on each other and love each other through thick and thin even after fighting with each other on a daily basis.

CARRIE STEINWEG

So, with National Sibling Day as a reminder, take a minute to let your siblings know how special they are. Chances are, they probably know how you feel, but an extra "Thank you" or "I love you" never hurts.

They grow up in a blink of the eye

April 30, 2006

    I don't think there's a parent out there who isn't amazed at how fast the time goes and how quickly children seem to grow. One minute they're barely scooting around on their hands and knees with a bottle, then next thing you know they're toting a backpack and a lunch box and heading off to school. The years seem to pass in the blink of an eye.

    For a child, it seems to work quite the opposite. Time usually drags in the eyes of a youngster. When you tell a child about something that's a week away, it seems like an eternity to them to get to that point. Back when I was a little one, I remember how I'd long to be older. I couldn't wait until I could ride a bike or until I'd lose a tooth. Then I couldn't wait to be in junior high and set out with my friends to the movies or the mall. Then it seemed I'd never get to high school or get my driver's license or graduate. It seemed I was always tapping my toes impatiently wanting to hurry up and hit the next milestone.

    Now that I'm a parent, I wish I could hang on to those milestones and special moments and just freeze time. I savor each one before the next one comes rushing around the corner.

    As a mother of five, I've witnessed so many milestones come and pass so quickly. As the aunt of 15 (soon to be 16) nieces and nephews, I've also watched them grow and have marveled at how they've changed. The oldest of them is my 27-year-old niece. It was quite strange becoming an aunt at just age 5 and she was often more like a sibling than a niece. The youngest of my nieces and nephews is my sister's 9-month-old little girl. In the middle are five more nieces and eight nephews.

Most of my nieces and nephews live in the Chicago suburbs or Northwest Indiana. Only the youngest one lives out of the area in Central Illinois, but I still see her frequently. Over the years I've seen them all fairly often, but in between visits I'm always surprised at how much they've changed.

I remember baby-sitting several of them as a teenager and changing the diapers of these little ones who are now in college and high school. I always loved being around kids and loved spoiling them when I got the chance.

When we married and moved to Lansing, we bought a house just down the street from my brother and his three daughters, so I got to see them quite a bit and we had a lot of fun times. I relished the role of "cool aunt," taking them out for pizza, stuffing them with sugary stuff and having sleepovers. I'm appalled when I think of the times I'd let my nieces stay up until after midnight as we'd watch scary movies, when I sneaked one into an R-rated movie she wanted to see as a preteen, when I assisted one in decorating the house of an ex-boyfriend in toilet paper and when I helped one ditch class so she could go to the beach. What a bad aunt I was!

As I recently watched as the youngest of my brother's girls, a high school senior, helped lead her basketball team downstate, I couldn't help but remember the times I dressed her up like Garth from "Wayne's World" and had her reciting lines from the movie when she was in kindergarten, when we'd jump together in ball pits and when I'd paint her nails. How she so quickly went from that to the 6-foot-tall beauty she is now is unbelievable. And with 11 nieces and nephews younger than her and five boys of my own, there are many more surprises to come.

Moms make the world go 'round

May 14, 2006

Sure, love makes the world go 'round and money plays a part, too, but where would we be without our moms? I don't mean to slight dads in the equally important role they play in their children's lives, but since this column happens to be appearing on Mother's Day, I thought it was only fitting to give moms a little credit for the tireless, often unnoticed, 24/7 duties that they fulfill for their little darlings.

Really, without mothers, who would make sure you wash behind your ears? Who would cut the crust off your PB & J sandwiches? And who would clean your dirty socks?

Ok, you'd probably run some soap and water behind those ears at some point. You might have to pull off the crust all by yourself or, God forbid, actually take a bite of it. And maybe your socks would get dirty enough that they'd walk to the washing machine on their own. Hey, stranger things have happened.

So, why does it feel different when Mom is the one taking care of those things? Moms have a way of making you feel loved even when they are doing such menial tasks as contemplating whether to use Tide or Shout on those filthy socks. They make you feel warm and fuzzy when that PB & J is served on a plate cut in perfect, crustless triangles. And admit it, no matter how much you complain about the nagging, you feel safe and secure with the woman who insists that the back of your ears are spotless.

Our moms take care of us from head to toe when we enter this world and slowly, but surely, we figure out how to do it on our own. Eventually, we even acquire the capability to do it for another human being and we enter the world of parenthood.

I've learned a thing or two from my mom's 51 years of parenting experience. I'm not just talking about learning to tie shoes or clean up your own mess. My mom, like every other mother out there has taught me many life lessons. Here are a few:

If you haven't got anything nice to say, don't say anything at all. Mom has always believed that you shouldn't call others names. You shouldn't gossip. You shouldn't say things you'll regret later. When my brother was a child and she heard him call his brother a name, she told him the word was unacceptable and that if he was unhappy with his brother, he could think of something else to say. From that day on when someone made him angry, he spouted out the word "trombone."

You can never praise someone enough. Mom disapproved of us saying crude, hurtful or mean-spirited things. The word "hate" wasn't allowed. And as much as she thought those words shouldn't be part of our vocabulary, she believes more strongly in complimenting people every chance you get. She believes that you should think twice before saying negative things, but should never hold back something good. She taught us to look for the good in things and to spread those good feelings.

Everyone needs a hug every day. It applies whether you're five or fifty. Life is better if you have someone in your life who loves you and shows you affection. Don't let a day go by without hugging your kids or telling them that you love them.

If you look for the good in things, you'll find it. Someone may look at a patch of grass full of dandelions and violets and give it a scowl, dismissing them as troublesome weeds. Mom would look at that same patch and rave about the beautiful, bright yellow and purple colors and how well they complimented each other.

Appreciate the little things. Things sometimes go wrong, despite our efforts and good intentions. So, when things go good, we shouldn't

MOM MOMENTS

take them for granted. Enjoy the singing birds and the sunshine, be thankful for the good homemade meals on your table and appreciate those special people in your life, especially your mother.

Don't make fun of mom jeans

May 23, 2006

The past few years I've been watching as the waistline of women's jeans and pants has gotten lower and lower. It didn't affect me much because I've spent much of the last few years in old maternity pants. I was shocked when the style in maternity clothing also become having the waist of the pants buttoned down below the belly instead of a strand of elastic sitting high above where your waistline used to be.

Now that I've said goodbye to my maternity wardrobe and the jeans that have seen me through my past few years have seen better days, I've been on the hunt for a comfortable and stylish pair of jeans and am finding out that it's almost impossible to find jeans that fit both criteria—at least for a body that's had five kids.

In conversations I've had with other mothers, there's a big joke about "mom jeans." Once you've had a few kids, you can't escape the fact that the most comfortable and best fitting jeans are the ones that snap in the area of your belly button, allowing you to hide that pouch that often remains across your abdomen after pregnancy.

Of course, this doesn't apply to all moms. There are plenty of thin, fit moms who can still wear an itsy-bitsy, teeny-weeny bikini without anyone realizing that they are a mom of three. I, however, am not one of them. I'm one of the many moms who has a little too much junk in the trunk and a little too much tummy spillage to be seen in a pair of capris that sit way low down on the hips.

"Mom jeans" could be compared to the slacks you see old men wearing hiked up almost to their armpits. They're not nearly as attractive as a snug pair of Levi's, but they're comfortable and most people reach a time in their life where comfort takes precedence over style. I hate to admit that I'm reaching that point already.

The "mom jeans" come from a Saturday Night Live skit, which of course exaggerated the denim pieces to make the waist of tight elastic, therefore accentuating the tummy bulge and padded behind. I haven't worn anything that extreme, but if I could find a way to keep my six-year-old Gitano jeans in good condition, I'd wear them forever.

I guess what bothers me most about the current style is that it's a sure signal that I'm getting older. I remember the days when I was rail thin and could wear anything without a visible bulge. Those days are gone.

The low waist jeans are meant to accentuate that area. I know my limits. There's nothing in that area that I want to accentuate. Thankfully, I'm aware of it. It wouldn't be a pretty sight.

I became painfully aware of that when I recently visited Old Navy to pick out some summer clothing for the boys. I figured I'd stroll over to the women's section and pick out an outfit for myself as well. I entered the dressing room with 12 items and couldn't find one that looked even close to appropriate.

Not only do the clothes come in "low waist," but also "ultra low waist." Those are the ones that you don't dare bend over in. The real zinger came when I asked the young employee if there was anything in the store that didn't have a low waist. She smiled and directed me to some that were labeled "just below waist" and explained that they used to sell "at waist" jeans, but they don't carry them anymore. Even the "just below waist" didn't cut it for an old lady like me.

So, I'll continue on my quest of finding a comfortable and stylish pair of jeans. Until then, please don't laugh at my "mom jeans."

The nursing days are numbered

June 11, 2006

    With my youngest of five now walking around and talking in gibberish, it's becoming sadly apparent that my days of mothering babies is coming to a close. Even after doing it five times, I can't get enough of snuggling with newborns, rocking them until they drift off to sleep and sniffing those freshly bathed baby heads. That precious first year goes way to fast. And now that my little one's made his way past the one-year mark, it also means the end of breastfeeding, which I've found to be one of the greatest joys of motherhood.

    For a lucky few, breastfeeding comes naturally and they're able to pull it off without much difficulty. However, for the majority of moms it gets off to a rocky start and is something you have to work at to get it to work for you and your baby. And just because you're doing it the second or third time around doesn't mean it will be effortless.

    Breastfeeding is something I'd encourage any mom to try. I fully understand that some moms have difficulties that prevent them from breastfeeding even though they want badly to experience it. Other moms have varying reasons that they would rather not breastfeed. If it's something you truly have an aversion to, your baby will sense that and will likely be unpleasant for both of you. I can only say from experience that I'm so glad that I chose to breastfeed my children. I would have been missing out on a beautiful bonding experience that cannot be matched.

That's not to say that it was easy. My first son spent his first 10 days in the neo-natal unit. While he was being fed special formula, I was pumping and pumping. Before he came home from the hospital he was being fed the pumped milk. Once he was home, we learned together. Having gotten started on formula at the hospital, I found I wasn't able to produce enough for him, so I supplemented with formula each day. It wasn't the natural process I'd envisioned, but I was happy to have some success at breastfeeding.

When my second son was born, he spent several days in special care due to a severe case of jaundice, which is believed to possibly be worsened by breastfeeding. So, it was back to pumping to ensure that my milk came in and the supply continued, although this time it all got dumped down the sink. Eventually he came home and seemed to take to it fine, until his skin seemed to still have that yellow glow and he was alarmingly lethargic. It was back to the hospital and back on the formula. Eventually, the jaundice was gone, he was back home and nursing became a pleasant routine. He also was supplemented with formula since I wasn't able to produce enough milk for him.

The third time around I had a healthy son who I breastfed throughout my stay at the hospital. This time I expected it to be easy, but somehow, I forgot how to hold the baby correctly (so did my friend who delivered her fourth one an hour after me and was in a room down the hall) and ended up in a lot of pain.

By baby number four I finally got the hang of it. Even through a hospital stay myself, I managed to pump to retain my milk supply (which had to be discarded because of the strong antibiotics I was on) while my husband gave him formula at home. By the time I got to number five, I was a pro.

Since becoming a mom, I've spent five and a half years breastfeeding babies. Five of those have been in the last seven years. I always get laughs when we're at a party and I'm offered a drink that I have to decline. I then explain that I haven't had a drink since the summer of 1998 because I've been pregnant or breastfeeding ever since then. I've gotten many offers for a free margarita to "celebrate" when I'm finally "free." I have such a hard time looking at it that way.

It will be strange to have my body back. No thinking twice before drinking a caffeinated beverage or eating dairy products or broccoli that will upset the baby's tummy. I'll be able to buy a real bra again, one that isn't a contraption of hooks, snaps, flaps and openings. But I'll be giving up much more than I'm gaining. Never again will I be able to gaze into my baby's eyes during a late night feeding. I'll be closing a chapter of my life that I'll never be able to revisit. So, I'll really be savoring these final days of breastfeeding. I know my nursing days are numbered.

Enjoying America's past time

June 20, 2006

I remember my first baseball game like it was yesterday. I was 10 years old and my father and twin sisters set out for Wrigley Field. I remember parking in what I seem to remember being a convent where parking in the lot was reasonably priced and then walking a couple of blocks to the ballpark with posters in hand. I even remember the blue shirt I wore that day with the words "Bleacher Bum" across the front.

I was so excited to see my idols in person—Ryne Sandberg, Ron Cey, Andre Dawson, Keith Moreland, Jody Davis, Rick Suttcliffe, Bob Dernier and others. It was the bunch who the following year would show promise of making it into the play-offs for the first time in 15 years.

I can remember taking it all in—the sound of the organ, the sight of vines of ivy moving with the cool Lake Michigan breeze, the smell of the steamed hot dogs, watching the guys peeking their heads out between the openings on the manual scoreboard. It was a time when you didn't have the choice of going to a day or night game. They were all day games. It was a time when you could expect the seventh inning to be interrupted with an often-off-tune but lovable Harry Caray spouting out "Let me hear you—A-one, A-two, A-three." There was nothing like it.

I remember just the anticipation of making my way up to the gate. People were crowded, moving down the sidewalks like ants dressed in blue and white—sometimes with some red trim. Men peddled peanuts outside the park. I remember being awed at the talent of the musicians playing on the surrounding streets.

Now I'm taking my little guys to Wrigley Field for the same experience, my most recent visit being last week. It's different now. Sometimes the games are viewed by light and although you still sing along during the seventh-inning stretch, it doesn't sound quite the same.

However, some things don't change. That ivy still sways in the wind. The scoreboard is still manned by humans, not a computer. The overpriced hot dogs still smell and taste great. It doesn't even matter if they win or lose. Cubs fans are no strangers to defeat. There's still nothing like a day at Wrigley.

However, I have come to really enjoy U.S. Cellular Field at night. Having been raised as a Cubs fan, I have never paid to go to a Sox game, but when I'm offered free tickets, I can't pass them up. There are a lot of nice features to attending a game there. It's closer and parking is more convenient. Overall, it's pretty kid-friendly. On our most recent visit on Cinco de Mayo, we enjoyed a mariachi band and spectacular fireworks after the game. It doesn't have quite the charm of Wrigley Field, but how can you not have fun seeing a World Champion Chicago team play?

It's now been 23 years since I attended my first baseball game and there's still nothing like it. And now that I've got a son playing Little League, it doesn't matter if I'm sitting in a green, metal chair within the Friendly Confines or on a cold bleacher outside a local field. Baseball is baseball. It makes you feel good

It's great to get away

June 25, 2006

During my past 12 years of being a parent, we've taken many family trips together. Some have been due to travel writing assignments. Others have been just because we wanted to get away or there was a place we wanted to see.

Many of our trips have been weekend getaways around the Midwest, but we've taken a few adventures that have taken us a little farther. I'm usually the one who makes all the travel plans, so it was nice this time when my husband planned out the trip and made the arrangements.

As I'm typing this week's column, I'm in a rocking chair on a balcony high in the hills looking out over Sevierville, Tenn., which is just north of Pigeon Forge and Gatlinburg near the Great Smoky Mountains National Park. My 2-year-old is napping. My husband is enjoying the jacuzzi, the baby is toddling at my side and my three oldest boys have just finished a game of air hockey and are heading into the hot tub, which is right by my side on our cabin's lower floor balcony. I'm a long way from home in miles and mindset.

We're nine days into our vacation and it's going to be hard to head home. Today has been our "lazy day." After several days of running, driving and sightseeing in South Carolina, we arrived at our cabin in the smokies last night and have spent the day chilling out at the cabin. It seems our trips are always so packed with activities that we often don't get any rest until we get home, so this time we built in a day where we would go nowhere.

The past week has included days at the beach digging for shells, visiting theme parks, riding boats, seeing many types of animals, dining out, shopping, playing games at arcades and swimming. Instead of getting up in the morning and rushing to feed children and get them to school on time, my morning ritual became an early morning ride on a golf cart with whichever child woke up first and an arm full of crackers, bread and cereal to feed the mallards and geese, accompanied by a gang of goslings.

Some days the hours have flown by with time running out on us before we knew it, other days time seemed to go slowly and the daylight seemed never-ending. Some days it didn't even matter what time the clock said. One day blended into the next with no inkling of what the date was. Even though we had a rough itinerary of things we planned to do, the pressures of the daily schedules disappeared.

Well, the sun is setting and I've got a little boy challenging me to a game of pool. Even though I haven't stepped out the front door all day, it's been a busy (but relaxing) one.

The testosterone is rubbing off

July 9, 2006

I knew it would happen eventually. How can you live in a house with six males and not, in a way, become one of them? Sure, deep down in me there is a feminine being who would love to go get a makeover and go on a shopping spree for things that are frilly and floral in shades of lavender and blush, but I've resigned myself to the fact that my day to day life will most days be more like spending time in a boys' locker room than at a spa.

I learned years ago when I began dating my husband that when you love someone, their interests become yours. I found myself really paying attention to cars, memorizing the body styles and makes and models. It was fun going to antique car shows and admiring restored vehicles we'd see on the street.

Not everything my husband enjoyed was as exciting to me, but I took an interest, even if I wasn't thrilled about bouncing around in a Blazer on a muddy trail off-road or freezing my buns off on a snowmobile on a bitter winter night in the middle of a forest preserve or pulling some slimy creature out of a grungy pond on a pole. I figured I could at least give such things a try and make the best of it and I usually had fun even if it wasn't my first choice of recreational activities.

I couldn't ever see myself remotely interested in doing a job that he did, but I'd ask about his day, hearing about welding or conveyor belts and later air packs and fire engines. It was part of his day and I liked hearing about it.

Now, years later, I find myself in a home with as much testosterone as you'd find in a hardware store. And it scares me a little when I notice how much it's rubbing off. I knew it was inevitable, but it's still a little unnerving at times.

One morning recently, I was the first one out of bed, which is quite unusual. I figured I'd take advantage of the few moments of peace and quiet. I plopped on the sofa and grabbed the remote. That alone should have been a hint. In many households, the men guard their remotes as if they are priceless jewels and mine is no exception. I grasped the remote, which doesn't fall in my hands very often, and held it tight as I began flipping through the many channels.

Ten years ago, if I was alone with a remote in my hand, I'd be inclined to stop on a dramatic movie, a prime-time soap opera, a talk show, a rerun of the Brady Bunch of the Wonder Years, a biography, a music video. It could have been a number of things, but it wouldn't have been primarily male-oriented.

On this particular morning, I passed up the cartoons (you'd be surprised how often I find myself watching Arthur or Spongebob after the kids have cleared the room.) I also went by the Lifetime movie and the Oxygen channel. I even passed up the Food Network. Suddenly I found myself flipping back and forth between an action movie from the 1980's starring Arnold Schwarzenegger and an episode of American Choppers. I did that for a good half hour.

Truth is, I'm enjoying the male-targeted television more than I'd like to admit. My boys wouldn't cuddle on the sofa with me to watch an episode of 30-minute meals or Oprah, but they're more than willing to sit on my lap and watch Trucks or Extreme 4X4 (I love the show's female host.) Same goes for a NASCAR race or a baseball game, a low-budget Sci Fi flick or an old episode of the Incredible Hulk, a monster truck event or a tractor show on the farming channel. And anything that will help me get some cuddle time is okay with me, even if it reeks of testosterone.

Are you a "pack rat" parent?

August 6, 2006

With the recent heat wave we've had, I spent a few days in the house (since it was just too miserable to go out) doing one those chores that I hate to do, but absolutely have to get to a few times a year—cleaning out closets and drawers. I really do like to organize things and when it's all done, I feel good about what I've accomplished, but the act of discarding of things is often painful.

When I started on this project, I had to admit to myself what my husband has been telling me for years: I am a pack rat—a major pack rat. I looked at several items and thought, "Why am I holding on to this?" Other items I knew belonged in the garbage can, but had a hard time parting with them.

I guess my problem is that I'm too sentimental. I remember distinctly where and how I got most items. If it was a gift, I remember the occasion and the giver. If it was something I purchased, I remember where it came from. If it was something the kids played with, it reminds of that time in their lives. Thus, I attach certain memories to things and it is hard to get rid of them.

Sometimes I'll keep some junky little ring that came out of a gumball machine, but when I come across it, I'll remember the time I was shopping at the grocery store with my son and he took a quarter out of his wallet and gave his special prize to me and that memory just makes me light up. To me, throwing away that little piece of junk, means discarding that special memory. It's coming across it buried in the drawer that provokes the memory. Without that little token, there's nothing to trigger that memory and it's gone forever.

I know I'm not the only parent out there who has this problem. I've talked to other moms who have expressed how agonizing it is to place a special art project in the garbage can that their little one has put so much effort and love into, but there just isn't enough refrigerator and wall space to display every drawing ever made by your child, so much of those precious pieces of art go into the round file or the recycling container.

It's bad enough that I hold onto things of my own that I really don't need to, but now I hold on to so many of my children's possessions that would probably never be missed if they suddenly disappeared. Even so, I keep hanging on to these things that make me smile.

I hardly ever wear jewelry, but I've got a jewelry box filled with items. None of them have much monetary value, but they're priceless to me, like the necklace and earrings given to me by my former co-worker, Jeannette, to wear to prom or the imitation pearls given to me by my sister-in-law when I stood up in her wedding. And, of course, a handful of gumball machine rings and bracelets.

I'm also bad about clothes. It doesn't matter if they don't fit and never will again. In the back of my closet, you'll find a dress that I put on my favorite doll, Emily, when I was a child. There's also a dress that I wore for my bridal shower 15 years ago and t-shirts I purchased on my honeymoon.

My recent cleaning spree included emptying out our "junk drawer" in the kitchen. I think every household has one of these. It's the place that you dump little objects when you don't know where else to put them. Among its contents were tokens to a now closed arcade, 14 bookmarks, a pair of broken sunglasses, pieces to a Scrabble game. They were all things that I easily discarded, but for each thing that made it's way into the garbage, there were two things that made me smile and got tucked back into corners or rearranged on shelves, so I really didn't make a great deal of progress. Am I running out of storage space? Definitely. However, the things I insist on keeping are things that for one reason or another make me happy. Why would I want to throw that away?

Each stage of parenthood has its rewards

August 20, 2006

There are many pivotal moments in parenting when you realize your child is moving on and growing up a little. It begins with the many "firsts" of babyhood. The first smile. The first steps. The first words. Then the first steps turn into sprints and the first words grow to sentences. One leap rolls into the next.

You know that these advances are inevitable and you look forward to them, but once they happen and you look back, it seems as if they've occurred so fast. As a mom of five, I'm in a unique situation. Just a few months ago I had an infant, a toddler, a preschooler, a grade-schooler and a middle-schooler all at the same time. Now the baby is a year old, which I guess moves him into the toddler category and the toddler is now three, technically a preschooler. It's fun to be able to witness so many different stages in the boys.

My youngest, now 16 months, is running all over, climbing, feeding himself, throwing a ball, dancing and babbling. He's so much fun. He still clings to mommy and reaches out for me to pick him up. When I do, he puts his head on my shoulder and stretches his arms across my shoulders and squeezes. Then as I pat his back, he does the same to me. It just makes you melt. He changes every day, saying a new word or doing something else to surprise me.

My three-year-old is changing at a rapid rate, as well. He delights in having conversations and asking questions. He wants to help mom do everything, yet he doesn't want any help himself. He's learning to be appreciative and grateful. Every day he thanks me for something I wouldn't expect. One day it's, "Thanks for making me dinner." Another day it's "Thanks for giving me a hug." He's turning into a little man before my eyes.

My four-year-old is the friendly, crazy one who is always laughing and wanting to make everyone else laugh. He's been a pretty independent child for some time and in the past few months has learned so much. He's writing words well and spelling some words. When he's interested in something, he just studies it over and over. When it comes to sharks or the human body, he can't see or hear enough. He recently took his second trip through the Body Worlds exhibit, a collection of actual human specimens that has traveled to different science museums around the country. While even his older brothers were a bit squeamish and scared, he was fascinated.

My seven-year-old is more quiet and reserved, but very sensitive, thoughtful and loving. I've been proud of how responsible he's been with our new puppy. He's always making sure he has toys and treats and he feeds him and takes him outside with being asked to. He enjoys learning and recently asked if I'd show him how to do some cursive writing and requested that I sit down and do math with him on a beautiful summer afternoon. He's also growing physically and doesn't need mom to get him things. He has a system of perching himself up on the counters without a stool to get a cup or a snack.

While I've noticed so many signs in my little guys that they're growing up, it's become most apparent in my oldest son, who is now 12. He just keeps getting taller and is within just a few inches of me. His voice has changed. His skin has changed. His arms have become more defined. Although he technically isn't a teenager yet, all the signs are there.

He likes to spend time in his room, going through baseball cards, reading magazines and downloading songs onto his iPod. He's more vocal about what he thinks is fair and what's not. He hasn't quite hit the stage yet where I'm a total embarrassment and he still likes to spend time with me shopping, watching television or playing games.

MOM MOMENTS

If there's one thing I'm learning as I stumble through parenthood, it is that there are many stages and phases that come and go and each one has its own rewards.

9/11 FALLEN FIREFIGHTER REMEMBERED OFTEN

September 3, 2006

Christian Michael Otto Regenhard is a man who I never met and who lived hundreds of miles away. However, he's someone I think of often. Here's why.

On September 11, 2001, I woke up feeling nauseous, fatigued, achy and swollen as you might expect from a woman who was 8 months pregnant. Although I only had about four weeks left of work before going on maternity leave, I felt lousy enough to stay home and use a sick day.

After my oldest son was off to school, I got in the shower. A few minutes later, my husband stuck his head in the door and said that my sister called and said to turn on the television because a plane had struck the World Trade Center. I hurried out of the shower. I've never been to New York and didn't know anything about the towers or the area. I sat in front of the television and watched in horror as another tower was struck and each came crashing to the ground.

I didn't know one person who was directly impacted by the terrorist attacks on 9/11, but like most other Americans, I felt such a sense of sorrow and just sobbed for days.

My due date was October 15, 2001. I hoped my baby, which we knew would be a son, wouldn't arrive on October 11, 2001. I just didn't want his birthday associated with the one month anniversary of those horrific events (like I had any choice in the matter.) I loved the name

MOM MOMENTS

Carter and we were pretty sure that Carter would be our son's first name. We were still mulling over middle names. We'd come up with a list of two dozen or so that we were considering. One of them was Christian.

On September 24, my husband and two older sons weren't home and I turned on the television to watch the prayer service that was taking place at Yankee Stadium. As the camera panned around the crowd showing somber faces grasping photos of loved ones missing in the disaster, for just a couple seconds it focused in on a woman holding a large picture of a young firefighter. Underneath the photo was the name "Christian." I knew right then that I'd found our son's middle name.

Carter Christian arrived on October 11, 2001. I remember watching the television in my labor room that morning as the president spoke and asked for a moment of silence for all those lost exactly one month earlier.

Although I knew nothing more about this man except that he was a firefighter missing in New York on 9/11, I thought about him often—whenever I'd say or write my son's full name, when I'd look at the calendar on the 11th of the month, when something would come on television about the World Trade Center towers. Earlier this year, I thought I'd do some looking on the Internet to at least learn his full name. Within a couple minutes I'd found a site listing the 343 firefighters lost on 9/11. I read each name on the list until I found the first name Christian. There was only one with that first name, Christian Michael Otto Regenhard. It also had his picture.

Just this week, I thought I'd try to find out more than just his name. An Internet search brought up numerous articles on his memorial service and his mother's attendance in hearings related to 9/11 and the organization she started in Christian's memory, the Skyscraper Safety Campaign (skyscrapersafety.org.)

I learned that Christian had just graduated from the fire academy in July of 2001 and was a rookie, or "probie" in firefighter terms. He had served five years in the U.S. Marine Corps and had traveled to 22 different countries. He was a hero whose life ended way too soon, like so many others that day.

Big fuss over a little one's meal

September 17, 2006

For a while there, it seemed that each day I opened the paper, the Back Talk section had one or more comments about public breastfeeding. It seems to have died down now, but I wanted to weigh in on the topic.

I remember writing a column back in 2004 when legislation had been proposed giving mothers the freedom to breastfeed in public in Illinois, thanks to Kasey Madden. Madden contacted lawmakers after she was asked to leave her health club after breastfeeding her daughter in a childcare area at the gym.

She wasn't removing her entire blouse in the middle of the weight room. She was discreetly breastfeeding her daughter in a separate childcare area. The law since has passed giving women the right to breastfeed in public places in Illinois.

I wrote in my previous column that I've breastfed all my children and there have been times that I've been out in public with a hungry infant and had no choice but to feed him in an area where there were others around.

I'm sure there were plenty of people who walked by and never noticed what I was doing. Whenever I could find a private place to nurse, I would. I'd often feed my children in the back of my van with the shades pulled and have been pleased to find a few places that have had nursing facilities, although there have not been many.

MOM MOMENTS

I can recall three museums that had a nursing room and a special area at the Illinois State Fair one year with rocking chairs in curtained areas. I've turned clean, roomy restroom stalls into nursing areas by pulling a chair into them to avoid making others uncomfortable. I once heard a mom say, "I wouldn't eat my dinner in a bathroom, why should my child have to?" and that certainly made sense.

It just seems odd that in a society that encourages mothers to breastfeed due to all the medical and financial benefits, there are so many people that will so passionately argue that a woman shouldn't breastfeed unless she's in the privacy of her own home.

Breastfeeding is a natural and beautiful process. Why should women be made to feel as if they're doing something wrong? An August 2006 article in Baby Talk magazine listed the reasons mothers don't nurse longer. The American Academy of Pediatrics recommends that mothers breastfeed their babies for at least a year, but many don't get to that point and one of the causes listed was negative public attitudes. Twenty-two percent of moms who responded to a survey said they were made to feel uncomfortable at some point.

And to address all the complaints in Back Talk that moms should simply pump their milk to feed their baby in a bottle, it's not as easy as it sounds. First of all, pumps are expensive, either to buy or rent. Pumping is time-consuming—one session of pumping usually takes at least 30 minutes. Also, a pump expresses less milk than a baby eats, so it often takes two pumping sessions to produce enough for a meal.

Pumping also can alter milk production, because the pump expresses less milk, so substituting feedings with pumping can decrease milk supply. Then there's also the issue of keeping the milk cold for transport, yet warming it for the feeding. It's a bigger hassle than some might realize.

I also agree with those who responded in Back Talk that people see more of a breast on television shows and commercials than from woman breastfeeding. I know I saw more bare breast during Janet Jackson's Super bowl half time show than I've ever seen from a breastfeeding mother.

What's in a Nickname?

October 1, 2006

Naming a child is something that parents take very seriously. Many often consider the possible nicknames that could accompany that name when deciding what to call their child. Michael may be shortened to Mike, Robert often becomes Bobby, Rob or Bob and a Christopher will likely be called Chris at some point. Katherine might become Kathy, Katie or Kate and other names like Elizabeth have many possibilities from Liz to Beth to Besty.

Sometimes parents prefer a shortened form of the name more than the name itself and decide early on that Isabella will be called Bella or Maximillion will go by Max.

Sometimes as the child grows older, he or she decides that a nickname is preferred and decides on his own to be called by something else. Many people often take on the middle name, or the parents even give the child a name intending to call him or her by his middle name. There are many reasons that people are born with one name and end up being called or calling themselves something else.

In my mom's family of six, only one went by her given name. John William became Johnny Bill or Jay, Richard Eugene went by Gene, and Nelson Orn somehow became known as Pat. As for the girls, Myrtle Ellen went by Ellen, while my mom, Kathryn May has almost always gone by Kathie and sometimes Katie May. Her sister, Lora Nerine is the only one who has been called by her given name, although people often call her Lori, rather than Lora. My mom's mother, who was named Carrie Ena, was always called Ena. In my dad's family of four, his brother Dennie Rex has always used the name Rex, while the others go by their given names. If you go back further generations, there are many more examples.

I have five siblings and four of them are usually called by a nickname that is a shortened form of their name. Michael is Mike, Pamela is Pam, Rebecca is Becky and Jennifer is Jenny or Jen. This happens in many families.

Then there are other nicknames. The ones that people get based on their personality or appearance (Red, Slim, Shorty.) The affectionately given ones that come from grandma (Sweet Cheeks) or the strange or silly ones that come out of nowhere from a crazy relative (Bozo, Bubbles). The unwanted ones that are given by the school bully or that happen to rhyme with your name. (One poor soul that I went to grammar school with was forever known as Tony Bologna.)

Sometimes nicknames are temporary. Sometimes they stick. One of my sons was called Pumpkin as a baby. Another was called Peanut. Each of them outgrew those cute nicknames by their first birthday.

One niece of mine got the nickname Booshie as a baby, which from what I understand came from the polish word for grandmother, "Busha." She's now 25 and I rarely call her Colleen. She's always Booshie. Her older sister, Kelly, was Kelly Bo Bean or sometimes Kelly Bo Bean Banana Bana Fo Feen or something like that. Thankfully, that nickname disappeared long ago.

Almost everyone has had a nickname at some point, given by a family member, a friend or a co-worker. For years my husband was called Junior, which was a sensible nickname since he had the same name as his dad. Some of his family members called him junior, but the nickname was used mainly when my husband and his dad worked at the same company to avoid confusion. It's been years now since I've heard anyone call him by that nickname.

I've had two nicknames in my life that I can remember. One, Baby Doll, was used just by my parents and they still call me that once in a while. The other was given to me by my big brother. I think it somehow came from the little bird that was Snoopy's buddy on the Peanuts cartoons, Woodstock. Maybe I got it because we had a dog named Snoopy when I was little. I don't think it was after the huge Woodstock Festival in 1969, but it could have been. My older brothers are the only ones who've ever called me that and once in a while still do.

So as the Tweeters, Sports, Princesses, Angels, Bubbas, Tigers—and Baby Dolls and Woodstocks—know, sometimes the nickname has more meaning that the one you're given at birth.

MOTHERHOOD CHANGES EVERYTHING

October 15, 2006

No matter how much you think you are prepared for becoming a mother, you just don't have a clue until that baby is plopped upon your chest for the first time. And even then, you don't have any idea how much there is to learn and how much your life will change.

You immediately notice how your life has been altered as your needs are instantly moved to the back burner to tend to the every need of your newborn. Everything is turned upside down, but it's a small price to pay for the beautiful little being that is now the center of your universe.

As time moves forward, you are reminded often how different life is as a parent. In your previous life, you didn't have someone spitting up on your shirt. You didn't care about the price of diapers. You didn't worry about SIDS. Diaper rash was the farthest thing from your mind. It didn't matter if you ate dairy products or chocolate or had a few cocktails, you weren't thinking about the contents of your breast milk. You could have cared less about the comparison between bouncy seats. Suddenly, these things and many others are weighing on you mind.

There are so many little things that you learn as you go…how to change a diaper by nightlight at 2 a.m., how to hold a baby to help him burp, how to remove poop stains from a white Onesie, how to suction the boogers out of her nose with that bulb thingy, where the little spot is on baby's foot or hip that elicits a squeal. And although so much is thrown at you all at one time, it doesn't stop when baby learns to sit up or crawl or walk or talk. Parenthood is a learning process that never ends.

Every day there is something that reminds you that you're a mom, no matter how far away your child is or how far removed you are from your domestic domain…the sippy cup that sits in the cup holder of your SUV, the pacifier that you find when reaching into your pocket for your keys, the melted fruit snacks that you discover when you reach in your purse for your checkbook.

One morning recently, I was out running errands by myself. I usually take this opportunity to find something on the radio that I like and I turn it up a little louder than usual. About 20 minutes into the trip, I realized that even though there were no children present, I was half way through a Wiggles CD. That's not the worst part. I didn't immediately turn it off. I was really into the song and finished singing along to "Dorothy the Dinosaur" before switching to the radio. Only a mother would do that (and probably a few dads.)

Becoming a mom not only changes our routine and our lifestyle, but in most cases, it changes the way we see the world. Those motherly instincts kick in to try to catch a child who you see is about to fall or to try to help a child who is distraught. The world all of a sudden seems bigger and you want to draw it all in teach your child all the good there is and protect him from all that is bad. And even when you're doing a superb job, you never feel like it is good enough.

And as each day moves on you learn just a little bit more about how to handle the challenges that come with motherhood. You also learn each day that there's still a lot more to learn.

Boys are from Mars, girls from Venus

October 29, 2006

I grew up in a girly house. My sisters and I did all the typical girl stuff—Barbies, dress up, tea parties. We had visions of marrying Prince Charming and moving into our pink mansion with accompanying horse barn.

We were polite, for the most part. We enjoyed setting the table properly. We sat with our legs crossed. We said excuse me if a burp managed to slip out of our mouths.

My dad adapted well to a house full of girls and served as a pretty good role model. He didn't smoke or drink or curse. He never displayed any kind of macho tendencies. He didn't have a dirty, physically demanding job where he was surrounded by macho men. He was an accountant and usually worked alone at a desk. He's an intellectual who taught us to read and love learning. He expected us to be as smart as he was. He rarely raised his voice. Most requests made by mom and us girls were usually happily filled.

I also grew up around my three nieces, which was more of the same…Barbies, dress up, make-up.

Becoming a mother to boys was completely foreign to me. I had no inkling what to expect. In my mind a good boy was one who was smart and acted smart. He wasn't loud. He wasn't aggressive. He was never mean. He had good manners. He avoided confrontations. He listened. He didn't contradict things. He didn't question things. My expectations were totally unreasonable. I guess my determination of what a boy should be like was a combination of my father's gentile characteristics and what I saw in childhood male classmates that I didn't like.

It really did take a while for me to figure out that there is a big difference between boys and girls. Boys play differently. Boys express things differently. Boys learn differently.

When my son was a baby, I insisted that we'd never have toy guns for him to play with. Now, over a decade and four more boys later, I've realized that boys can make a weapon out of anything, even something as harmless as an empty paper towel roll or a feather. And I've seen more excitement in their faces during a water gun fight than I ever had playing dress up.

I've seen a lot on television and read a lot lately about the different learning styles of boys and girls. Many experts are even recommending that boys and girls be educated in separate environments that are more conducive to their learning styles. Girls are more apt to sit quietly and listen to a lesson, while boys often need to be more active and learn things better in a more hands-on environment.

I also watched a program recently where a set of boys and a set of girls were given paper and crayons to emphasize their creative differences. The girls used many colors and made flowers and rainbows. The boys used just a few dark colors and drew action scenes—an alien falling from an exploding UFO, a crashing car, a war battle with soldiers shooting at bad guys and scenes of that sort. I had never realized how normal it was for boys to draw pictures of racecars crashing or people bleeding. I've always chastised them for depicting anything violent and encouraged them to draw something "nice."

Raising boys has required many revisions to my earlier thoughts about the male gender. They're rougher and tougher. They're louder. They're physical. They're competitive. And despite all that, they're still totally lovable.

Riding the rollercoaster of behavior cycles

November 12, 2006

I once read a book on childrearing where an expert mentioned how behavior in children rotated in six-month cycles. Basically, what he said was that a child who is a terror at age 3 will transform into an angel at 3 ½ and vice versa. I must say that I have found this to be true for the most part. I've noticed that their behavior seems to go in cycles. The phases don't always last six months, but are pretty close. I'll have a few months of remarkable behavior followed by a stage of temper tantrums, outbursts, moodiness and general uncooperativeness.

However, since I have five children, I never seem to get them all in the phase of near perfection at the same time. One is going through the phase of having fits, while another one or two are perky and polite and another one is on the verge of cracking or returning from the dark side.

I might have my seven-year-old willingly giving his toy to 3-year-old brother, who in turn throws it across the room, stomps his feet and erupts into tears. My five-year-old will tickle his 18-month-old brother and talk to him in a sweet baby-talk tone only to have the baby scream in his face and run away.

Of course, every day is different and there are so many variables. Less sleep aggravates the crabby ones, a sunny day produces smiles, a delayed meal-time prompts a meltdown.

In the past couple weeks, I've seen the dark days of my 3-year-old come to a climax and he's suddenly waking up in a cheery mood, he shares without suggestion and the affection is constant.

At the same time, my darling youngest's angelic stage had been going on for quite some time and I was overdue for a move in the other direction. Now that it's time to cycle into the more undesirable behavior, it's a doozie. I've never had a child who has objected to having pictures taken in a studio, but when I tried to get his 18-month photos taken recently, he wouldn't let go of me and just screamed as I tried to place him in front of the camera.

His first word was "yeah," and that was his response to almost everything. If he wanted something, he'd point and say "yeah." Most questions were followed by, "yeah" or silence. The word "no" has finally made it into his vocabulary and it's never said calmly or quietly, it's blurted in a load, shrill screech.

So, while I'll be basking in the lovable stage of one, I'll be suffering through the not-so-lovable stage of another. But, there's always a silver lining. It should only last another 5 ½ months.

Curls aren't just for girls

November 26, 2006

My two oldest sons are blond with green eyes, just like my husband. They were both born with a head full of hair, but it was very light, very fine and very straight. Their cute blond locks later became bowl cuts and eventually buzz cuts. My 7-year-old still wears a buzz cut, while the oldest prefers the shaggy look of hair creeping over his ears and the back of his neck.

It was quite a shock when my third little guy was born with red hair. Although I was born with very dark hair, it lightened as I was a baby and developed some red highlights, so I guess the red hair came from me. His hair is also very straight and is worn combed to the side. Ask him and he'll tell you it's brown. I guess he's tired of all the comments about his unusual red hair at just age 5.

My fourth son is like the older ones with fine, straight hair that is very blond. My youngest was born with brown hair, which has lightened quite a bit since birth to a dirty blonde. What's different about him is that as his hair started growing out, I noticed how it was starting to curl on the ends. I just love babies with curly hair, so rather than cut it all off, I've merely trimmed it in the back and kept those adorable curls.

This hasn't sat well with my husband. Even after he's just gotten a trim, my husband asks when I'm going to give him a haircut. In my husband's eyes, he looks too much like a girl with the ringlets hanging from his head, and he'd rather my son's hair be shorter.

It doesn't help that every time we go out, someone tells my husband what a cute little girl we have. It doesn't matter if he's dressed in blue from head to toe, with a sweatshirt that says, "Little Slugger" on it, people still look at the curls and assume he's a girl.

I know that once those baby curls are chopped off, they'll probably be gone forever. I don't intend to keep them growing until he looks like Tiny Tim or Weird Al Yankovic. I just want to enjoy the baby curls a little longer.

Maybe I can copy the big name designers and make him his own t-shirt for Christmas with an appropriate slogan. How about black cotton that reads "Curls aren't just for girls?" Maybe that would help alleviate the confusion.

First snowfall brings blizzard of fun

December 10, 2006

The first snowfall each year is a pleasant occurrence in our home. My little ones eagerly await that first accumulation of snow, hoping that it's the right consistency for a snowball fight or a snowman.

A little over a week ago, the weather forecast was warning a doozie of a storm would result in up to 12 inches. So, after hearing reports all day long of what we'd be waking up to, the boys prepared by digging out boots and snowsuits that had been packed away for months.

It seems so often the weathermen predict inches of snow and it somehow seems to miss us in Chicago's south suburbs. Suburbs to the north and west are buried in white stuff, while we see just flurries. Northwest Indiana and Southwest Michigan get pounded with wind, sleet, slush and snow and we'll have just a slight dusting.

Some would say we're fortunate not to be the recipients of the brunt of the storm. We're spared from driving in it and having to shovel it. However, for a kid who hasn't seen a snowflake in nine months, it's a big disappointment when a snowstorm passes us by.

As I suspected, we awoke to find only an inch or so of snow on the ground, but that was enough. My kids woke with smiles on their faces, raced to the window and looked out in amazement.

Breakfast and school were the farthest things from their minds. My 7-year-old and 5-year-old were in their winter gear and in the back yard within minutes making snow angels. The 3-year-old was anxious to join them, but was denied the privilege after causing some major plumbing headaches by flushing a new bar of soap down the toilet—just the fourth time in a month.

The 5-year-old was on a mission. I watched out the window as he completed his snowman and began looking for sticks for arms, a carrot, hat and other items. When he was done, he stood in front of the snowman and extended his arms out. He didn't move. A few minutes passed and he stayed in the same spot without moving an inch. A few more minutes went by. Still, he didn't budge.

Finally, I poked my head out the door and asked him why he was standing there. His reply: "The sun is out. I'm blocking him so he won't melt."

What a difference a year makes

January 7, 2007

The holidays are behind us and we've said good-bye to another year, but there's much to look forward to, especially when you're a mom.

The past year has brought many changes in my little guys. When 2006 began, I was the mom of a baby who was just starting to crawl. He was learning, but not yet getting far.

I could still place him on the floor in the middle of the room and he'd scoot and spin and roll and occasionally get up on his hands and knees, but wasn't yet making it across the room.

A year later he's a big ball of energy—running, climbing, reaching, talking. It's amazing the number of changes you see in a child that age. A few months later when we took a vacation to South Carolina, he took his first steps after walking along the furniture for weeks.

Once on the beach, though, he would do anything to keep his feet from touching the sand. It was also on vacation when he slept through the night for the first time in 10 months. After months of sleepless nights and many ear infections, he had minor surgery to insert tubes into his ears. It worked like magic and within a couple weeks he was sleeping through the night again.

At the beginning of the year, he was making sounds, but not much that resembled real words. Now he is constantly babbling and his vocabulary has grown from one-syllable words, like mom, dad, car and milk, to pancake, backpack, cereal, computer.

While the year began with strained peas and squash and baby biscuits, he's now got a mouth full of teeth and has moved to regular table food. Some of his favorites are macaroni and cheese, grapes, asparagus, mashed potatoes and Nutter Butters.

He's gone from two or three power naps a day to just one afternoon nap. He's starting to dress himself. He's building towers with blocks. He "reads" the newspaper, although it's always held upside-down.

He's helping with clean up, depositing toys in the correct container. He recognizes everything you say. A mention of the word "going," "ride" or "bye" prompts him to run out of the room and come back with shoes in hand. He's running with the big boys, flopping, crashing, diving, wrestling and laughing the whole time.

What a difference one year can make. It's been an exciting year and with a whole new year before us, there are lots more changes to come

I MISS THE LUNCH BREAK MOST OF ALL

February 4, 2007

These days, I spend most of my time taking care of children. I prepare meals. I clean up after meals. I change diapers. I do dishes. I do laundry. I read books. I help with homework. I dress little ones. I vacuum. I drop off kids at school. I pick up kids from school. I schedule play dates. I help out in the classrooms. I shop for groceries. And I do a variety of other motherly chores, each day being different from the next. In little pockets of time in between, I manage to do some writing.

Up until about four and a half years ago, my days were much different. For my first eight years of being a mother, I was a working mom, except for maternity leaves.

At the time I left my full-time job, I was a mother of three, and I'm now a mother of five. I got up in the morning, would help get breakfast on the table and the little ones dressed. Then I'd head off to work.

There were many things I enjoyed about my job. It was close to home and very convenient, and I didn't have a long commute that took away more time with my kids. It was a very friendly place to work; I had great co-workers, many of whom I still keep in touch with.

Although I hated wearing nylons when it was cold outside, it was nice to dress in something other than sweatpants and worn-out jeans.

I worked as an administrative assistant to the human resources director at a high school district and I truly loved my work, whether it was organizing things in the office, working on the computer or dealing with people.

There was satisfaction in completing a project, whether menial or complex. I could schedule an appointment, or I could prepare a teacher contract based on a one-semester contract with a three-fifths class load in dual departments at step Master's-plus-15 on the salary schedule with five years of teaching experience for a new hire and file it away.

Some projects were ongoing, but most had closure. (There is no closure with laundry and dishes.)

With that said, the thing I really miss most about the working world is having a lunch break. That short span of time allowed me to relax and run errands.

When I began freelance writing, I often used the time to do phone interviews and meet deadlines. Some days I'd go shopping or run out for fast food. Some days I'd sit in the lounge and chat with co-workers. Other days, I'd read a magazine. Whatever I chose, the time was all mine, and no one ever followed me into the bathroom begging me to open a juice box or turn on "Blue's Clues."

Moms like snow days, too

February 18, 2007

Aaahhh! The pressure was off.

I had just gotten the phone call confirming what I suspected—and what I secretly hoped—that school was not in session the next day (Valentine's Day.)

I was watching the 9 p.m. news the night before and noticed that just about every other school in the area was listed for school closings, but my second-grader's school wasn't on the list.

I'd already gotten the call that my middle child wouldn't have preschool tomorrow, which took away some of the guilt of settling on the sofa to watch "American Idol."

This time it was my son's friend's mom calling to say she was told by the lunch lady who was told by the principal that school was closed the next day—music to my ears.

While I do feel bad the Valentine's parties wouldn't go on as planned, I was relieved at not having to set the alarm, drag the kids out of bed, bundle them up, warm up the van, head out in the cold and maneuver the sloppy, icy roads to get to the schools for drop-off and party time.

A burden suddenly was lifted. No lunch to make, no outfits to get ready, no Valentines to gather and no party supplies to prepare.

When I left the morning before on what should have been a 25-minute round trip to drop off my 3-year-old at preschool, it turned into 45 minutes. The roads weren't too bad early in the day, so I ran the last-minute errands for Valentine's treats. By pick-up time the wind was blowing more and the streets were getting slick. When I went to pick up my second-grader at 2:40 p.m., I was moving like a snail and still having trouble. A five-minute drive took almost 20 minutes. I was glad I wouldn't have to deal with it the next day.

I can remember it like it was yesterday, being a child watching the snow fall outside the window and hoping it would be enough to close the school. So many times the winter storms weren't quite bad enough to call off classes, and we'd grumpily head out the door listening to stories about how our parents walked miles to school in worse snowstorms.

On the rare occasion that a snow day was called, it was always a day full of fun play at home and some rolling around in the yard making snow angels.

Even when snow isn't the cause, it's always refreshing to have a day off from the regular routine. I really looked forward to not having to leave the house at all. I thought I'd catch up on some paperwork, maybe cook a pot of soup, light the fireplace and spend some time chilling out with the boys. It's an opportunity for some quality time that often seems so hard to come by.

New world view with exchange students

February 27, 2007

Last summer my sister saw a newspaper ad seeking a host family for a Japanese exchange student for about six weeks. She agreed to host the girl, named Ayaka, who moved in with her, her husband and her 1-year-old. She was also expecting another baby at that time.

My sister enjoyed the experience so much that when Ayaka moved on to Seattle to study there for the school year, she decided to host a different Japanese girl, Yukiko, who was arriving here for the 2007-08 school year. She also persuaded a neighbor to also host a teenage girl from Japan. In the fall, my sister decided it would be nice to host a second exchange student to be company for Yukiko and the two reviewed applications for teenage girls coming to the United States for the second semester of the school year. They decided on a girl named Christina from Germany, who arrived about a month ago.

Since my sister became so familiar with the process of placing exchange students, she was asked if she'd be interested in working as a local coordinator by assisting in placing students arriving from other countries and helping American students wishing to study in other countries. I thought I'd include this information for anyone in the area who would be interested in hosting a student in their home or who has a child considering studying overseas.

The agency that she works with is Academic Year in America, www.academicyear.org. It works with students coming to the United

States from several different countries and works with potential host families willing to take a student into their home for either a semester (five months) or a full school year (10 months.)

Host families are able to choose the gender and nationality of the student and some home countries include Albania, France, Macedonia, Tajikistan, Argentina, Germany, Malaysia, Thailand, Armenia, Hong Kong, Moldova, Turkey, Austria, Hungary, Mongolia, India, Philippines, Uzbekistan, Indonesia, Poland, Ukraine, Brazil, Japan, Venezuela, Bulgaria, Italy, Romania, Vietnam, China, Japan, Russia, Chile, Columbia, Korea, South Africa, Ecuador, Kyrgyzstan, Spain, Egypt, Luxembourg, Switzerland.

You can also select the age of the student between 15 and 18 1/2, which works well if you have a teenage child and would like them to be in the same grade. My sister said that some host families seek out students with the same interests as their children, such as sports or dancing. The program is not open only to families with teenagers. Younger couples and senior couples can also host a student.

Students come with their own insurance and spending money. Host families are required to provide meals and a bedroom, which can be shared with a host sibling of the same gender within four years of age.

I'm always interested in learning about other cultures and this seems to be a great opportunity for both sides to learn a lot. During my freshman year of high school I recall having exchange students from Sweden, Germany and Russia in some classes and I though it was fascinating.

Tech memories make a mom feel so old

March 4, 2007

Recently, my husband and I reflected on how much things have changed since we were kids.

Our oldest son is now nearly 13 and the world seems so much different than it did when I was that age. The more we talked, the older I felt.

I remember when cassette tapes were cutting-edge technology. When I was a young child, we listened to records and 8-track players. Now, even compact discs are disappearing as everything is downloaded.

When we were young, the word "digital" was used in reference to a clock, but now it means something entirely different.

I remember getting our first microwave oven. It seemed so strange to make popcorn without popping it on the stove. My kids have never known life without a microwave. I remember when we still had a rotary phone. I was probably in third grade when we got a push-button phone. My husband remembers when his home phone was on a party line shared with neighbors.

I got my car phone in the early 1990s, and it was called a "car phone" because you could only use it in the car. It had a big bag attached to it with a battery that was larger than the phone itself.

I was in grade school when our 13-inch black-and-white television quit and we replaced it with a HUGE 19-inch color Zenith model.

I also remember when we invested in a Beta VCR and how amazing it was to record episodes of "Growing Pains." I still remember when we first got cable television and that my dad would not let us watch MTV. It amuses me that MTV, which began as a round-the-clock music video channel now has more shows and commercials than music videos in its programming.

I think I was about 12 when we got a Nintendo Entertainment System as a gift from my uncle. Compared to the Atari games I'd played at my friend's house, Duck Hunt and Mario brothers seemed out of this world. I just can't get used to the graphics on the games these days.

I didn't own a computer until 1992. My 386 hard drive cost about $2,300. My dot matrix printer required sliding the connecting paper over the holes on the side and then tearing apart the perforated sheets when it was done printing. In high school I learned to type on WordStar, do spreadsheets on Lotus and create a database on D-Base.

It makes we wonder what it will be like when my grandchildren laugh about old-fashioned electronics or how lame reality television was.

'Babies don't keep' sound advice

March 18, 2007

More than any other words my mother spoke when I was young, those I remember best are "Babies don't keep."

It was the ending line to a poem on a plaque that hung in our home. She put the rhyme to music and often sang the words to us as she rocked us in her chair or as we'd sit on her lap. She'd hold us close and we'd use her chest as pillow as she'd pat our heads and sing the words.

"The cleaning and scrubbing can wait 'til tomorrow, For children grow up as I've learned to my sorrow. So, quiet down cobwebs and dust go to sleep, I'm rocking my baby and babies don't keep."

By the time I was born, she was fully aware of how quickly children grow up since she already had three teenagers, the oldest being 17. She had me a week before turning 37 and was older and wiser than the last time she became a mom at 23.

She was more experienced, more relaxed. She'd experienced a "natural birth" when I was delivered, which was much different from delivering a baby in the 1950s.

I was delivered by Dr. Carol Rawlins, a Northwest Indiana obstetrician who died recently and was a pioneer by making mothers active participants in the birthing process at a time when it was not yet common practice.

While formula feeding was the norm when she had her first three children, my mom breastfed me. I think all of these things made my mom look at mothering with great appreciation.

I've taken my mother's words to heart, and I try to savor each of those moments when my youngest (now 23 months) is groggy and lays his head on my shoulder or when my 3-year-old climbs into bed next to me early in the morning or when my 5-year-old lands in my lap and asks, "Mom, can I cuddle with you?"

There are undoubtedly always at least a dozen other things I could be doing at that minute, from washing dishes to folding laundry to vacuuming the floor. But while I know the laundry won't be going anywhere, I have just a small window of opportunity to use those moments to wrap my arms around my little ones and take it in before they're off and running again.

And who knows if that opportunity will present itself tomorrow?

So, if you happen to stop by and notice some cobwebs or a sink full of dishes, it's because it will be there tomorrow, but babies don't keep.

Road to independence bittersweet

April 1, 2007

There are many signs of growing up parents notice on a daily basis. Some are welcome and often long overdue, such as when our little ones learn to tie their shoes, use the toilet and sleep through the night. Those independent acts mean less work for mom and dad and that makes that little step toward growing up a little less heart wrenching than, say, the first time they walk through the doors of the school on their own, waving as they leave you.

Some subtle reminders can leave parents feeling torn—proud at their child's accomplishment or what they've learned, yet sad at the thought that one day they'll be out on their own and will no longer be depending on mom and dad as they once did.

I had one of those moments recently as I was walking through a parking lot with my 3-year-old and my 5-year-old. I insisted they each hold my hand.

My 5-year-old complied and then looked at me and said, "But mom, 5-year-olders don't need to hold hands anymore."

I instantly recalled a television interview I'd seen of Jamie Lee Curtis just after her children's book, "It's Hard to Be Five: Learning How to Work My Control Panel," was released. She explained the big transformation between a 4-year-old and a 5-year-old and talked about how you don't quite feel comfortable letting a 4-year-old walk by a street without holding his hand, but at 5 you have the confidence to let go and let him walk beside you without clutching his hand in yours.

I knew my son was right. I could trust him enough not to hold his hand. Although he had to still be by my side, I was confident he wasn't going to dart out or run the other way like his 3-year-old brother would likely do if I let him walk alone. I told him he could let go of my hand as long as he stayed beside me and watched carefully for cars.

I smiled as I watched him strut through the lot, acting as if he were not 5, but 45. That little bit of independence went a long way.

The fish are biting.

Routines help avoid 'evil' force of chaos

April 15, 2007

Parenting inspiration can come from many places. I've gotten bits of advice from other moms over the years. I've clipped magazine articles. I've dog-eared pages in parenting books. I've bookmarked Web sites with critical information.

I also like to collect quotes about parenting lessons and life in general and tuck them away. One thing I've heard over and over is the importance of routines from other parents and grandmothers, from pediatricians and professors, from authors of books about surviving the toddler years. Children want to know what to expect.

They like stability. They thrive on rituals. They often react better when there's a schedule to follow. However, I think it was expressed best not by a child-rearing expert, but by a favorite Disney character, Buzz Lightyear. In his own full-length feature film, Buzz Lightyear of Star Command said, "Procedure is what separates us from the wicked forces of chaos."

He, of course, was not referring to taking care of little ones, but to saving the galaxy from the manipulative claws of Emperor Zurg. However, the statement applies to life with a couple of youngsters. For without some sort of procedure in a house full of kids, chaos is likely.

Think about how haywire things go when you take a vacation with kids. While the days may be jam-packed with fun activities, mealtimes and naptimes get rearranged often resulting in a cranky child that could make the most self-assured adult flinch.

Bedtime is unpredictable—you either get a child who collapses from exhaustion or is wired beyond control. And once you return home from a trip it often takes several days to settle back into the routine.

I guess you could consider "managing chaos" as one of the duties on the parenting job description. For kids who get used to routines, straying from them can produce some unpleasant moments. Even on the good days, when the schedules are in place, you're often just one step away from chaos.

Take a 1-year-old to the grocery store at naptime or give a famished 3-year-old an Elmo plate when he always eats his lunch on a Blue's Clues plate, and you're asking for trouble.

So, whether you're a space ranger intent on rescuing some little green men from an uncharted planet or you're tackling potty-training, getting dinner on the table or bedtime, procedure can be your best friend.

Goodbye to a beloved aunt

April 24, 2007

Last week, our family lost another member, my mother's sister-in-law of Charleston, Ill. Both of my parents grew up in Charleston, my dad's home being just down the street from Eastern Illinois University. They moved to the Chicago area around 1970. When I was a kid, we usually made it to their hometown about once a year and would always stop to see my Uncle Gene (mom's older brother) and Aunt Carolyn and their family.

They always welcomed us with big smiles and hugs and greeted us with enormous hospitality, whether we had a day-long visit planned or if we were just popping in unexpectedly while in town. Their home is just about 2 hours and 30 minutes south and they always lived in a neighborhood, not in the rural outskirts of the town, but their whole family spoke with an accent different from what we were used to around Chicago. For some reason, I called it a country accent. Aunt Carolyn always just reminded me of a sweet lady from out in the country. She was as friendly as could be and seemed so content at home fixing supper for her gang. One thing we had in common was being mothers of boys. I have five. Aunt Carolyn was the mom of four boys and she unfortunately lost two of them before she herself left this world, peacefully in her sleep. Her son Bobby died in his late teens while he was in college and her oldest, Richard, who had served many years in the U.S. Army, died in his 40s.

It has been a few years since I've been to Charleston for a visit, but etched in my mind is the image of Aunt Carolyn greeting me at the door, holding my cheeks as she gave me a big kiss and calling me "sweetie." And before we'd even sit down she was offering a glass of iced tea and a piece of pie.

Thank God for ear infections and allergies

April 29, 2007

Sniffles. Tummy aches. Scraped knees. Ear aches. Every parent dreads the little everyday illnesses and injuries that make our little ones uncomfortable. But as I was thinking recently about all the people I've known who have endured things much more serious with their children, it makes me appreciative when seasonal allergies or a stubbed toe are the most serious health problems in our lives.

A former co-worker that I keep in touch with has had to deal with a daughter who was born with a heart defect. Her daughter underwent heart surgery just a few days after birth and again at age 2. She'll face at least one more surgery as she grows, but the operations have been successful and she seems to be a normal, happy preschooler. Her older sister, who has had occasional seizures during her eight years, is now facing the possibility of brain surgery. All this is going on while her mom battles cancer. I can't imagine what it would be like to be in her shoes.

I remember when my sister's good friends lost their son, who was about 7 years old. He simply went out in his yard to play in the snow. When he climbed over a fence to retrieve a ball, his scarf caught on the fence and he died.

There was the handsome college student, the brother of a friend of the family, who died on his way home from school when his car hit a broken-down truck coming off an expressway ramp.

A friend who had her first daughter not long before I also became a mom went to get her 6-week-old daughter from her crib after a nap and found her not breathing. She had died of Sudden Infant Death Syndrome.

I recall a couple that were good friends with my parents as I was growing up and had a teenage son with an undetected heart problem. He died of cardiac arrest at the wheel of a car not long after getting his driver's license.

When I was about 6 years old, a cousin who was close in age died along with his mother in an accident when the vehicle they were in rolled over.

I have a friend, now in her 70s, who lost a son to Muscular Dystrophy in his late teens. As a single mom, she lifted him in and out of his wheelchair to care for him, which I know was not easy for the tiny woman. I remember someone once asking her how many children she had.

"Three," she answered. "Two living on earth. One living in Heaven."

I'll also never forget being at a get-together at the family home of my sister-in-law when I was 9 or 10 years old. Her older sister, an accomplished pianist, sat on the bench beside me showing me some notes. She then went on to play a song that she'd composed, telling me she'd written it for her little boy who had died of SIDS.

When I think about all these families that have had to deal with serious illnesses or deaths of their children, I realize how lucky I am to have had to deal with not much more than a toddler with a broken arm and minor surgery to have ear tubes inserted.

Moms provide many memories

May 13, 2007

With my deadline looming, I was contemplating different topics for this column and then realized it would print on Mother's Day. So, I figured it would be a great opportunity to recall some of those special things about my mom and thank her for all she's done.

Mom has always loved to create special memories for her kids, and she always paid special attention to every detail. She has such a knack for decorating, something I never picked up. She was always thumbing through Better Homes & Gardens, House Beautiful and other magazines for ideas.

Growing up, our home was always full of plants. Mom especially liked hanging ferns near the windows. She's definitely got a green thumb. Again, not something I inherited from her. She made sure we always had a centerpiece on the table. Sometimes it was a bud vase with roses picked from the yard or a bundling of blooming branches from our forsythia bush in the vase my brother made in a college pottery class.

Sometimes it was an African violet she picked up at the grocery store. Other times it was seasonal; an arrangement of twigs and colorful leaves that had fallen from the huge maple tree in fall, a mirror with fake snow and ice skating figurines and snowmen in the winter. There was always something decorative in the middle of the table.

When it came to meal time, Mom worked hard to fix something good that included our favorites, and insisted we come to the table to eat the meal while it was "piping hot" and drink the tea while it was "ice cold."

It's been years since I've tasted a bowl of her delicious chicken and dumplings, potato soup or navy beans and ham with cornbread, but thinking about it now sure makes me hungry for it. I can almost smell it cooking.

It wasn't often that a new dish was introduced. Mom usually made the same dishes over and over, and they were ones we all loved—salmon patties with buttered potatoes and spinach, chopped steak with mashed potatoes and corn, pork chops and stuffing with peas, tacos, spaghetti with lots of meat in the sauce.

Once in a while she'd bake an apple, berry or rhubarb pie or some Irish soda bread for dessert.

She'd usually lead us in saying grace before dinner. We often had candles lit as we ate, and we almost always had cloth napkins rolled in rings that coordinated with the tablecloth.

Mom is very creative. She was always writing in journals and was editor of her high school newspaper, so that was one trait I did get from her. She's also a talented artist, and I recall her doing some beautiful drawings when I was younger.

Another talent she had which has slipped by me was sewing. She'd spend hours cutting quilt squares and sewing them all together on an old black Singer that I don't think was even electric. It had a foot pedal and some belts on it.

Whatever we happened to be interested in, Mom would show an interest. I remember when I first learned to read, I was crazy about the "Little House on the Prairie" series on television and started reading the books by Laura Ingalls Wilder.

Mom somehow found me a floor-length, pioneer-style dress and a matching bonnet that I'd put on whenever I would read the books. She went to great lengths to get us special things—a dollhouse, a playhouse for the backyard, a kitchen set, special dolls, and would scour garage sales and antique stores to find exactly what would fit.

MOM MOMENTS

One year just before Christmas, she had a winning lottery ticket that netted about $2,000 and she made sure I got an expensive leather coat I'd been begging for. I outgrew it at least a dozen years ago, but it's still hanging in my closet.

When I think back on all Mom was able to do as a mother of six, I feel like I've got a long way to go to accomplish half of what she has.

What was it Abraham Lincoln said? "Everything I am or hope to be I owe to my mother." I agree

I'M A MOM IN A BOY'S WORLD

June 19, 2007

It's strange for a girl who grew up with sisters to spend her days focused on boy stuff. My childhood revolved around Barbies and tea parties. These days my life is full of superheros and Hot Wheels cars.

From the moment I wake up, I'm surrounded by boys in Superman or Spiderman pajamas. They're loudly rolling cars across the floor and crashing them into something. And they're always getting dirty. In the summer months, it's not unusual for them to take two or three baths a day. One day last week I came home to find two of the boys sitting in the laundry tub sink with a couple of toads they'd found in the backyard.

And while there are some activities, like going to baseball games, that I enjoyed as a child and enjoy doing with my own boys (I have five of them) there are other more male-oriented activities that I've adapted to, like fishing and riding all-terrain vehicles.

Last week I took my boys to an event that I doubt I would have attended when I was younger. I spent a Saturday afternoon packed in a crowd of primarily sweaty teenage boys watching Tony Hawk's Boom Boom Huck Jam at Six Flags Great America. The event included professional skateboarders Tony Hawk, Jesse Fritsch, Sergie Ventura and Kevin Staab, BMX bike rider Kevin Robinson and MotoX rider Drake McElroy. During the show, the athletes performed choreographed tricks to music.

Ever since I watched the X Games with my oldest one a few years ago, I've been fascinated with watching skateboarding. At the time,

MOM MOMENTS

Shaun White (a.k.a. "The Flying Tomato") was one of the newer competitors and I could have watched him all day.

Seeing these pros up close was really impressive. Each of the tricks performed individually was cool enough, but then to watch them perform doubles routines was really amazing. I just can't believe how easy Tony Hawk makes it look. And although I kind of felt old in this crowd of teens, I was surprised to learn that three of the four skateboarders were older than me. Hawk just turned 39, Ventura is 36 and Staab is 41. So, having boys has opened my eyes to a lot of things in the world that I probably wouldn't have been interested in otherwise.

I'll always be Daddy's little girl

June 24, 2007

Last month, I shared some special memories of my Mom in a column that ran on Mother's Day. This month, I didn't have a column running on Father's Day, but I still wanted to share a little about my father.

At age 34, I think I'm more of a Daddy's girl than ever. I usually see my Dad a couple times a week, often when he comes over to watch my little guys for a couple hours so I can go to a meeting, help out in one of my kids' classrooms or go to the health club. Sometimes we talk on the phone and send each other e-mails.

He calls when he has a funny joke to tell me or to chat about an extraordinary ball game that he watched. I call him to share something cute that one of the kids has done or when I make some extra chili or meat loaf for him and Mom.

We go together to plays, concerts, movies, sporting events. Once in a while, we go out to eat or shop together. We have political discussions and now that I'm all grown up, I feel comfortable disagreeing with him.

No matter how big you get, you can recall the day when your Dad was the only knight in shining armor there was. Mine is no exception.

It was evident to me back then that I was the apple of his eye. Well, one of them. I'm one of six kids, so I was not the only one he admired.

However, he's always done well at making each of us feel special. For years, the joke among my sisters is how he tells each one of us "Don't tell your sisters, but you're my favorite."

Some of my earliest memories of my Dad are of us sitting at the table as he showed me homemade flashcards and I recited the words. Dad also had a huge dictionary on a podium in our living room and whenever we heard a word we didn't recognize, he'd send us to the podium to look it up.

It made me feel pretty important teaching my classmates words they didn't know and impressing my teachers with five-syllable words in third grade.

Another great memory with Dad was on Sunday mornings when "The Lone Ranger" would be shown on WGN. The credits would roll and the "William Tell Overture" played as the Lone Ranger bounced on the back of his horse, Tonto. Dad always bounced me on his knee all the way through the song.

I remember putting on fancy dresses and standing on top of Dad's feet while we waltzed in the living room, making snowflakes out of tissue paper for winter decorations, mixing iced tea together and watching him install a pond and waterfall in our backyard.

My dad is one of the calmest, kindest, most sensitive men I know and I enjoy getting to know him more and more as time goes on.

Horoscopes can provide laughs for moms

July 8, 2007

I'm not one who reads horoscopes regularly or necessarily believes the three lines I'm reading actually apply to me (and also the other millions of Leos out there.)

For the many years I worked in an office, a coworker would cut out the horoscopes and pass them around so everyone could read what was supposed to be in store for them that day.

It definitely was entertaining and funny to see them sometimes ring true. And it was often that something rang true precisely because of its vagueness.

Several years ago, I was glancing through the paper and just for fun looked up my horoscope. I laughed out loud because it fit me to a "T"—not only that day, but pretty much every day and not just for me, but probably for most mothers of young kids.

Here's what it said: "It is likely that you could be saddled today with a plethora of unpleasant tasks to do because of hanging out with dependent individuals who can't fend for themselves."

I clipped out that horoscope and hung it on my fridge. When I occasionally glance at the horoscope section now, I read not only my sign, but others and see how many lines could apply to a mom. There are always several.

For instance: "Change doesn't happen overnight." "You enjoy receiving a lot of attention, but it's a distraction." "Let go of illusions and remain firmly rooted in the here and now." "Revive your own spirits by being loud and clear about your beliefs." "Try to see the forest instead of just the trees." "There may be a necessary trade-off of independence to achieve cooperation." "Someone might surprise you by doing something nice." These are all ones I found in a recent horoscope column.

Sometimes on the days when you're saddled with a plethora of unpleasant tasks to do because of hanging out with little freeloaders, such lines can shed some light on the situation or put things into perspective—or at the least, give you a much-needed laugh.

A BIRTHDAY WE SHOULD REMEMBER

July 10, 2007

    Today's date probably doesn't have a lot of meaning to most people unless its significance is related to an anniversary or birthday within your family. However, it's a day I want everyone in our town to circle on the calendar and remember. It should be a significant day to everyone in Lansing.

    On this day in 1981, a boy named Philip J. Martini was born. He would later become LCPL Philip J. Martini, serving in the U.S. Marine Corps. He was a son, a brother and a friend to many. He's not the only person from Lansing to serve his country in the Iraq War, but he's the only one who has died in doing so. His life ended much too soon on April 8, 2006.

    I never had the opportunity to meet Martini. I have been lucky enough to meet some of his friends and classmates who also have served in the Marines. I've also kept in contact with one of his brothers, Anthony. In his most recent e-mail, he wrote about how difficult it's been for his family. The reminders that he is not coming home have been ongoing—the anniversary of his death, followed by Memorial Day and Independence Day and then his birthday. Anthony said that this fall Phil would have been discharged from the military and the buddies he enlisted with will come home.

    "The family is still moving along. Some days are tougher than others" Anthony said. "I'd just love to buy him a beer and have him celebrate that birthday with me, even if I only had five minutes," he explained and he also reminded me to "count your blessings because you don't really know what you have until its gone." Earlier this year as the Bears were heading to the Super Bowl, he e-mailed and said that the day of the last Bears playoff game was the last time he saw his brother alive. Phil had decided to skip his flight and go back a day late so he could see the game with his family. "We all thought he was crazy for missing his flight to watch the game but in retrospect I'm glad he did because even though the Bears lost, I'll always remember that day," he wrote. On what would have been Phil's 26th birthday, Anthony will be running with bulls in Pamplona, Spain. "I have always wanted to backpack through Europe but until now I have always had an excuse," Anthony explained. "Well, Phil's death has taught me that you've got to live your life and damn the consequences. To me, it's a proper tribute." So, whether it's a silent "Happy Birthday" or "Go Bears!" or raising a beer in his memory or running with the bulls, find a way to remember and recognize this son of our community who gave his life for our country. And then count your blessings.

Aging pages bring past to life

July 24, 2007

For nearly 10 years, I've been a member of the Lansing Historical Society and for several of those years I volunteered once a month as a docent at the museum in the library's basement, opening doors for visitors, answering questions and pointing out interesting pieces in the exhibits. These days I'm not there as often, but I fill in when needed. Last week I was there to work and as usual, I found myself enthralled with information and the two hours flew by.

For several months, volunteers have worked tirelessly to preserve about 50 year's worth of old Lansing Journal newspapers that have been crumbling in storage. The papers are bound in books, but the goal is to scan each page so that there is computer access to all this information.

In the past, I've carefully turned the yellowed pages and was absorbed as I read about the nation's events, the local social scene and the prices in grocery ads. This time I was lucky enough to find some pages that had been scanned and printed and I started to thumb through them, this time not worried about cracking or tearing.

I was surprised to look at the stack and see several front pages of the paper from the 1930s and the one on the top of the stack was dated July 16, 1931. It was exciting to look down and have the news in front of me from that same date 76 years ago. The front page included articles on a proposed increase in railroad rates in Illinois and the discontinuance of two trains on the Chicago and Eastern Illinois Railroad, an announcement of the upcoming American Legion Edward Schultz Post picnic, details on the expedition of a Calumet City man to the far north out of Nova Scotia to explore biological growth and the story of a 5-year-old saved from drowning in the clay hole on Wentworth Avenue.

A 1933 paper's headline read "Hailstorm Sweeps Lansing Vicinity: Homes and crops damaged by storm of hurricane proportions." The storm knocked down 150 utility poles and caused $30,000 in damage to Lansing and the surrounding countryside.

The front page of a 1934 edition included the death of 15-month-old Alice Lucille Vroom, who died at home from heart trouble, the 50th wedding anniversary of Mr. & Mrs. John Kemp and a New Year's Eve Fireman and Policeman's Ball that raised $10 for each department. The fireman's portion was donated to buy books for Thornton Fractional High School after a recent fire.

I read about the 1938 Lion's Club Halloween activities, which included a pig greasing game where the kid who could catch the pig won him as a prize and the christening of Carleton David Beckman in an English service at St. John Church.

I just read and read—about funerals that took place in homes and a junior high graduation with six members in its class. Phone numbers had three digits, a subscription to the paper was $2 a year and you could buy four tall cans of milk for a quarter and a peck of potatoes for nineteen cents. It was a nice way to spend a couple of hours and I can't wait to go back and do it again.

Moms enjoy movie time, too

August 5, 2007

Earlier this year, I realized how long it had been since I'd rented a movie that wasn't animated or rated PG. I made up my mind; once every week or two I'd rent a movie and instead of doing housework or spending time on the computer after the kids were in bed, I'd relax and watch a movie.

I've always loved going to theaters and getting lost in a movie for a couple of hours. As a busy mom, I don't get to do that very often and I'd forgotten how enjoyable it is to forget everything else and immerse yourself in the story on the screen.

I'm the type who gets totally invested in what I'm watching. If it's something scary, I jump out of my seat. I sob at heartbreaking scenes. I'm on the edge of my seat at something suspenseful. And, I hate to admit it, but I've even blurted out things to the characters on the screen. A touching movie often stays with me for weeks, entering my mind here and there as I go about my day.

Since starting this movie-rental routine, I've learned about the lives of others through "Ray," "Walk the Line" and "The Queen." I've rented comedies and chick flicks and those of a more serious nature, like "Hotel Rwanda" and "Flags of Our Fathers."

While the first goal of Hollywood is simply to entertain—and bring in millions of dollars—so many movies tell a story that needs to be told.

A trend in movies these days is to include several different storylines that intertwine. "Crash," "Babel" and "Syriana" are three powerful films I've rented recently that follow that method. Each gives a glimpse into different cultures, classes and races by telling several different stories and the domino effect of how one situation can change the outcome of several other situations.

While those movies dealt with some uncomfortable and touchy topics, I appreciate that they expose the viewer to issues and perspectives that you don't get in daily life. While keeping in mind that it is Hollywood and that material is often exaggerated and altered to make it more interesting, it provides you with a look at more than one side of the story. It gives a human side to those who we may see as evil and shows that the good guy isn't always motivated by noble intentions.

To the average person who isn't a world traveler, films like these take us to other parts of the world, and show us what causes people to do the things they do and the unfathomable hardships others face.

It gives us a little understanding and it is understanding that will help us look at people differently and see that they may be more like us than we think.

What only-child parents avoid

August 19, 2007

Recently, while remote surfing, I came across Bill Cosby in a comedy routine from early in his career when he had five young children.

He talked about the struggles, hassles and inconveniences of parenthood. It was interesting to listen to him talk about the old-school approach of physical discipline that was acceptable back then.

The part about parents of only one child not really being parents made me laugh. And, while a mom of one child is no less a mother than a mom of 10, there are some unpleasantries that mothers of only children are able to avoid, he reasoned.

So, for those who have completed their families with an only child or who have yet to add siblings, I'll let you in on a few things you're missing out on.

* When there is only one child, you know who to blame. There's no game of whodunit involved in finding out who decorated the walls with a violet-colored crayon. You can go right to the source of the artwork and it's a done deal.

* The first words uttered by a first born are often "Mama" or "Dada" or something cute. My eldest son's first word was "car." When you get to child number three or four, don't be surprised if the first words your hear are "mine" or "me first."

* There's no one to fight with. Your time spent as a referee is limited to time spent with cousins and classmates and they're more likely to be playing than fighting when they're with them.

* Why is it that a toy can be sitting untouched for weeks, but the second a child picks it up the sibling is suddenly interested in it? When there's only one, there's no one to grab it away and cause a crying spell.

* Having to have everything the same. I remember when I was growing up with two sisters close in age, we always had to have three of everything. My mom would buy three exact coloring books, three of the same-colored hair ribbons.

* Having to have everything different. Each kid is an individual and at some point you'll hear complaining about not wanting the same things as siblings and wanting to be different. You're darned if you do, darned if you don't.

* Someone's always unhappy. One day I told the kids we were going to the pool. One quickly ran and got his swim trunks on in total excitement, another begrudgingly put his on, and another refused to get dressed and left for the pool in long pants, socks and shoes and moped all the way there. You can't make everyone happy all the time.

* The younger ones grow up too fast. With my first one, I limited his exposure to violence, bad language and anything remotely inappropriate. Recently, my 2-year-old sat down and started watching "Ghost Rider" with my husband and eldest son.

"This is just wrong," I told my husband. "A 2-year-old shouldn't be seeing this, he should be watching Barney."

He agreed, but noted that while a 2-year-old wouldn't mind watching a movie beyond his years, you wouldn't get the 13-year-old to watch Barney.

* Moms of several kids often become skilled short-order cooks. With several different appetites and tastes, you can never make a meal that everyone will equally enjoy.

* Someone is always getting left out. Even moms who are expert multitaskers can't attend to the needs of four kids at the same time. One-on-one time is a precious commodity.

First day of school isn't easy

September 2, 2007

School is back in session now, but the past few weeks have been nerve-wracking. Besides getting through registration and working my way down the supply list (which often makes me feel like I'm on a scavenger hunt), there were first-day jitters, well, for me, anyway.

This year I have four kids in school, and three are attending new schools.

With my oldest, now a teenager, I worried about his making new friends, fitting in and being up to speed with the curriculum. And it's a tough age. You want to be there for them but not embarrass them.

It seems like yesterday he was starting kindergarten. I remember the day so well. My niece came over to babysit his little brother, so we could go alone to McDonald's for lunch before his half-day afternoon class.

I remember the cute, colorful outfit he wore and his coordinating backpack. I remember how his hair was combed and how he hugged me tight before I left his class that first day.

After we entered the room, he read some books to me and did some puzzles and then slowly inched away and started playing on his own. I realized it was time to go. I drove down the street and took a photo of the outside of the school for his scrapbook, my eyes tearing up as I looked through my lens.*

With my second son, age 8, starting his fourth year at the same school seemed old-hat. He was happy to have one of his buddies in his class.

My 4-year-old began preschool in a familiar and nurturing environment with a teacher he'd been around for the past two years when he joined his older brother at school.

But my third son, age 5, was starting kindergarten at a new school. Unfortunately, the school has a policy that forbids parents from entering school on the first day.

I was surprised when I walked in the door with my son and was scolded and told no parents were allowed in the building. It didn't make sense to me that parents who wanted to be involved were turned away and the children sent into an unfamiliar building full of people they'd never met before.

I didn't get to see his classroom or meet his teacher. I really missed not having the opportunity to have him show me his name on his desk or explore his new surroundings together.

My son went on to his class without a fuss, but I saw one boy outside the school sobbing. I felt sad this would be his first memory of school on the first day of his entire school career, being sent into the school crying while his mother had to stay outside.

I asked a friend who is an early-childhood teacher. Also surprised a school would implement such a policy, she wondered if a child who was having a hard time with separation might have a harder time on the second day because he couldn't get acclimated to his surroundings with a parent beside him.

In her classroom, she invites parents to stay with children the entire first day so parent and child can go through a day's routine together, easing the process for both. She even bakes goodies for the parents.

I'd love to have readers weigh in on this topic. What do you think of this policy? Did you take your child into the classroom on the first day of kindergarten? What kind of policy does your child's school have?

Today is Tuesday, Sept. 11

September 11, 2007

The last time Sept. 11 fell on a Tuesday, it began as a clear, sunny, warm morning and ended as the darkest day in recent American history. It was a day that removed our perception of living in a secure and peaceful time in our country. We realized that we were vulnerable and had enemies that would not hesitate to take lives, no matter how innocent or removed from their focus of vengeance.

Every generation has been affected by war in some form. Being born toward the end of the Vietnam War, I was too young to remember it. And as I grew up in the late 1970s and '80s, terrorism and war seemed only something that happened in far away places. I remember reading "The Diary of Anne Frank" for the first time as a young girl and then having trouble sleeping for days, scared that bombs would be dropped. When it finally sunk in that what I'd read had happened decades earlier and in another country, I felt at ease, perhaps with the notion that it couldn't happen here.

I was just out of high school when the Persian Gulf War began and then quickly ended. The war of my generation lasted just weeks, the ground war over in days. I naively thought that I wouldn't see any other wars in my lifetime. I didn't even realize there were extremist groups that would plot to kill large numbers of Americans. For today's high schoolers, it's completely different. In their young lives, they've seen our country attacked and their neighbors and peers go off to war. They live in a much different time.

MOM MOMENTS

The "new normal" means that Sept. 11 isn't just a day on the calendar. It's associated with the day that nearly 3,000 individuals died senselessly, not as the day that Hurricane Iniki hit Hawaii, Pete Rose beat Ty Cobb's career base hit record or actor John Ritter died, all also events that happened on Sept. 11 in different years.

Yet, in a way it is another day on the calendar. Life goes on and there are school and sporting events. People will be shopping, eating dinner and doing things that they do every day, but not in quite the same way they did on Sept. 10, 2001. Although memories of the day have faded, we can never fully let our guard down.

I prefer not to recall the tragedy as much as the amazing stories of those who miraculously survived or helped in every way they could. I remember attending a candlelight vigil at Memorial Junior High School days after Sept. 11 when people gathered to remember those lost and joined in public prayer. Through something horrible, people came together.

For some, our current days are times of discontent. We've grown weary of war. The losses grow as each day passes. If nothing else, we can look around and count our blessings and be sure that all that we do have in front of us right now is not forgotten. And that may be the best tribute of all.

Hats off to Grandma and Grandpa

September 16, 2007

Last Sunday was a day many people may not celebrate or even know exists—Grandparent's Day, an opportunity to celebrate some special people who often play significant roles in children's lives.

Unfortunately, I never had a chance to know my paternal grandfather, who died before I was born. My maternal grandfather died when I was a toddler; I don't remember him at all.

My maternal grandmother died before I was in kindergarten and since she lived far away, I'd only seen her a couple of times before her death. My paternal grandmother died when I was about 10, but she also lived far away and spent her final years in a nursing home in Minnesota. I remember she was diabetic, and my dad would let us pick out sugar-free candy at the store to send her.

I always felt left out as a child when other kids would talk about spending Christmas with their grandparents, going shopping with them or going on vacation with them. I always wished I had a grandparent living close by to spoil me.

My husband never met his paternal grandfather, who lived in Germany and never visited the United States. He died last year in his 90s. He met his maternal grandfather for the first and only time when he was about 30.

He was able to get to know his grandmothers. One lived in Germany and didn't speak English but made a few visits to the United

States. She attended our wedding, and it was such a joy to meet her. What we lacked in communication was made up for in affection. She was one of those grandmothers who smothered you with hugs.

My husband's maternal grandmother is still living, but lives hundreds of miles away and we haven't seen her in about five years. She's one of those feisty grandmothers you wouldn't want to approach if you were a purse snatcher. We don't see her often, but we enjoy her phone calls and letters.

I'm so fortunate both my parents and in-laws live close and are involved in my boys' lives. My father-in-law attends the boys' baseball games and stops over often to visit or work on projects with my husband. The boys occasionally spend the night at their house, and Grandma will do crafts or bake with them.

My parents live just five minutes away. My dad comes over often. The boys snuggle up on the sofa with him, and they pop in a movie or watch a Cubs game together with popcorn and iced tea.

Then the boys see my mom and dad when we go over to the house for our weekly game night. We usually order pizza and spend an evening playing Boggle, Password, Rack-O, Imagine-iff or another game and then dig in to dessert. The night is always full of fun and laughs.

I feel so lucky they're able to have these wonderful experiences with their grandparents that I didn't have as a child.

If you're lucky enough to have grandparents in your life as well, be sure to let them know how much they mean to you and your children.

Why it takes three hours to do the dishes

September 30, 2007

If you're a parent, delays and interruptions are everyday occurrences.

Little ones tend to distract you from household duties and demand attention or are eager to be helpers when you're in the middle of projects, which is a nice gesture but not always efficient.

Sometimes they contribute to your inability to complete what should be a five-minute job in less than three hours.

One day recently, as I looked at the clock, I had to laugh when I realized that I had been trying to do one chore for several hours and backtracked to figure out why it had taken so long.

The task was getting the dishwasher loaded.

Unloading clean dishes is my 13-year-old's regular chore, but it's rare that he notices it's full of clean dishes and ready to be emptied and does it without prompting.

I usually have to let him know it's time to do the job and then sometimes remind him to do it at least once.

After my husband left to drop the kids off at school, I realized the dishwasher was still full of clean dishes from dinner the night before. I considered letting it wait until my son got home from school to unload it, but the sink was filling up from from breakfast.

MOM MOMENTS

I pulled out a clean cup for some water and noticed it was time to leave with my 2-year-old and 4-year-old for a play group. I figured I'd finish the job when we got home. Here's what happened from there.

* 11:05—Returned from a walk to the library. Pulled out a couple cups from the dishwasher to pour milk for the kids. It's not quite lunch time, so I get out a snack. As they're eating the snack, I unload a couple plates.

* 11:12—I noticed the 2-year-old had finished his snack and was pulling out markers. I returned to the table to supervise and we pulled out paper. My 4-year-old asked for help spelling his name, so we spent some time making letters. Things seemed under control, so I went back to the kitchen and unloaded a few more things.

* 11:25—The boys remembered about the books they picked out at the library. We sat down and began reading.

* 11:40—After several books, they were distracted by some toys and I returned to the kitchen and put away some more cups. My 2-year-old followed me and wanted to put silverware away. As he put away spoons, I realized it was almost lunch time and started working on that.

* 11:51—I heard screams from the other room and went to referee. It was almost time for the Doodlebops, so I sat with them until it started and then slipped away to finished lunch and put away some bowls.

* 12:20—Lunch was on the table. They ate. I finally got the rest of the dishes unloaded.

* 12:30—More refereeing as I cleaned up the table.

* 1:05—I started to load the dishwasher. My 4-year-old brought me the mail, and we went through it.

* 1:15—I told my 2-year-old it was time for a nap; he stalled by munching on the apple he didn't finish at lunch. While he ate, I loaded a few more dishes.

* 1:20—I realized I hadn't eaten lunch and made a plate. I ate standing at the kitchen counter, placing silverware in the dishwasher in between bites. More refereeing.

* 1:30—I took the 2-year-old up for nap and continued loading dishes.

* 1:45—My 4-year-old asked if we could make some sun tea. We got that done and then played for a few minutes.

* 1:53—I returned to the kitchen and finished loading. Then I started going through some mail and paperwork and folded some laundry.

* 2:09—I realized I forgot to put in soap and started the dishwasher. It only took three hours and four minutes.

Your own personal history is priceless

October 14, 2007

I've written before about what a history buff I am. Many topics interest me—American history, food history, automotive history, architectural history, sports history, industrial history, local history.

I love studying about the past of people, places and things.

I also love to uncover bits of family history, like that my great grandfather was 100 percent Pawnee Indian; that I'm a distant relative of William Clark (of the William and Clark expedition); and that my grandmother and grandfather had to secretly marry in another county because she was a school teacher and didn't want to lose her job since at that time (1920s), only unmarried woman could teach at the local school.

A bit of a pack rat, my most meaningful possessions are those that have a bit of family history to them.

I have a varied collection of dishes from each branch of our families—a pink depression glass dish from my husband's maternal grandmother, a plate showing the Brandenburg gate in Berlin from my husband's paternal grandmother and aunt, a flowered serving plate that belonged to my maternal grandmother and a deviled egg dish and relish tray from my paternal grandmother.

There's also a lovely scalloped dish with a Victorian couple painted on it that was made by my father's sister and given to us as a wedding gift, a set of German steins from my father's brother-in-law who immigrated here from Spain and the set of dishes our family used when I was a child my mom handed down to me.

Other sentimental items include the Bible my aunt and uncle bought on a trip to Jerusalem and gave to me on my 13th birthday, the bracelet another aunt gave me when I graduated from eighth grade, a hedgehog doll my husband received as child from his German grandmother and my hand-made personalized Christmas stocking knitted for me by my great aunt Harriet.

Every family has such possessions, having no intrinsic value but making the owner feel rich nonetheless.

Two other items with a bit of family history we've recently added to the collection fit in this category.

One is the American flag that was placed on my husband's great-grandfather's casket. Unfortunately, I know little about him and will have to do some investigating. I'm not sure of his birth or death date, so I'm not even certain if he served in World War I or II. I look forward to learning more details about him.

The other item is something I stumbled across on the Internet after my father mentioned he had a great uncle who used to play baseball for the St. Louis Cardinals named Al Shaw.

My sister and I started searching for information on him, and it was such a thrill to read about his baseball career, which spanned 1907 to 1915.

I came across a Web site selling tobacco cards, which were small early baseball cards that came in tobacco tins, and I found one of Al Shaw that was not too expensive.

The card has obviously seen better days, but it's priceless to me.

What songs are in your soundtrack?

October 23, 2007

Music is a powerful thing. The melody can take you to another place. The lyrics can remind you of another time. I love all kinds of music. I recently realized how diverse my tastes are after we subscribed to Napster and suddenly just about any song—and several versions of it—was right at my fingertips.

It's funny how songs are attached to different memories. As I pulled songs into my playlist one night, it seemed as if I was creating a soundtrack of my life. I wondered what songs other people would select to make up the soundtrack of their lives. Here are a few of mine and the memories they invoke.

"Elvira" by the Oak Ridge Boys.
This is the first record our family owned that was something other than classical music. My sisters and I knew all the words and tried to make our voices as low as possible when singing it. It always makes me think of my mom because she liked country music (when country wasn't cool.)

"Unchained Melody" by the Righteous Brothers.
It was one of the songs I labeled as "our song" in high school. I'm not sure why. The lyrics didn't really fit. I think I just wanted to stake my claim to a Righteous Brothers song since my husband had once sang "You've lost that loving feeling" to an old girlfriend in the middle of White Castle like Tom Cruise had done in "Top Gun." We danced to the song at our wedding.

"Almost Paradise" from "Footloose."
This was the theme of my eighth-grade May dance. I wore the pink bridesmaid dress I had worn the previous summer at my sister's wedding.

"Who Stole the Kishka" by Frankie Yankovic.
I asked the DJ to play this at my wedding. I remember watching my neighbors Art and Effie Aylmer, and my co-worker Barb Askew and her date dancing to the song. I attempted to polka with my friend's sister.

"Love Me Do" by The Beatles.
I remember sitting in the kiddie pool at a water park on vacation holding my youngest when he was about 8 weeks old as I sang the song to him. He giggled uncontrollably like he never had before. I remember making a mental note to soak it up, knowing how quickly babies grow.

"Islands in the Stream" by Dolly Parton and Kenny Rogers.
I liked this song until my best friend's dad got the 45 and played it over and over and over day and night. Whenever I hear the song I think about him and how much fun he was.

"What a Wonderful World" by Louis Armstrong.
My whole family had gathered at my brother-in-law's house. He was dying of cancer. The room had cleared and it was just him and I and a commercial came on the television with the song playing. Tears rolled down his cheeks and he said "This song just makes you feel like you're a kid again." We hugged for a long time. He died about six months later. I cry every time I hear the song because it reminds me of him.

Safe Haven Law helps save newborns

October 30, 2007

Each year at Halloween, something comes to mind that I wrote about a few years ago. A newborn baby had been left on Halloween morning at an Orland Fire Protection Department firehouse. The baby was just a few hours old and a phone call alerted the firefighters that a baby had just been left outside.

That newborn boy was the 10th baby in Illinois to be safely surrendered since the state's Safe Haven Law was enacted. In the prior month three newborns died in Chicago after being abandoned or placed in dumpsters. The Abandoned Newborn Protection Act was signed into law in 2001.

The firefighters were thankful that the baby was left unharmed at the fire station. As one firefighter I talked to put it, he'd much rather find a newborn left at the fire station than to go to a call where one was found in a garbage can. Unfortunately, the second scenario is still happening. Since the introduction of the law, at least 42 babies have been illegally abandoned in Illinois and at least 21 of them died.

The law has, however, resulted in some adoptions to loving families, including the baby boy I mentioned earlier. Over the years, an additional safe haven location was approved, the number of days that a baby can be left has been extended and last year the law was added as part of the curriculum in heath education classes. The way the law stands today a newborn seven-days-old or younger can be surrendered, unharmed, to a hospital, emergency medical facility, police station or staffed firehouse. The baby must be handed to a staff member, but the person surrendering the baby can leave with no questions asked.

For more information on the Safe Haven Law, go to http://saveabandonedbabies.org or call (312) 440-0229. Women who need immediate help can call (800) 510-BABY.

Saying "Thank You" a Special Gift

November 25, 2007

"Feeling gratitude and not expressing it is like wrapping a present and not giving it."—William Arthur Ward

I love this quote and it is so true.

How often do we feel grateful for something someone has done, even if it was something small that might not have required a lot of effort, but was done with genuine kindness?

It probably happens several times a day. An elderly man holds a door open for you, another mom sees you struggling with you kids and tries to pitch in, your spouse gets you something to drink, your child gives you a hug.

Those two little words are nice to hear and nice to say. If you don't express gratitude when you feel it, you're missing a good opportunity to brighten the day of the person who brightened your day.

To me, the words "thank you" are some of the most powerful words you can tell someone. It lets them know they are appreciated, that you noticed their kind gesture or the good job they are doing; it provides a connection to another person.

I was always taught to be polite growing up. As a result, saying "thank you" comes naturally. It became habit to always say "thank you" when someone waited on me in a restaurant or when someone pitched in to help. Still, I sometimes overlook things and don't offer words of gratitude that are deserved.

Kids today have a much different upbringing from my generation and those before me. Most kids have way more material possessions than their parents did. They probably don't have to experience the hard labor previous generations did.

Sometimes it's hard for them to appreciate things when they don't realize how fortunate they are to have them. The lessons of gratitude catch on early when they are modeled for kids. It's heartwarming to hear words of thanks from your little ones.

My 4-year-old says, "thank you" all day long as I help him with things or do things for him. And my 2-year-old blends "thank you" and "you're welcome" together, telling me "thank you welcome" when I hand him a cup or buckle him into his car seat.

Expressing gratitude can really enrich your life. A few years back, my mom bought me a gratitude journal and encouraged me to end each day by writing at least three things I was thankful for that day.

There was never a shortage of things to write down and at the end of a busy day it reminded me to stop and smell the roses. Even during tough or turbulent times, writing down those things you're grateful for transforms your attitude and makes you see things differently.

So, while the past few days may have been filled with words of thanks and gestures of appreciation, let's remember to continue that throughout the year and give thanks when it should be given.

Why wrap a gift and not pass it on to be opened?

A mom's Christmas wish list

December 24, 2007

Forget diamonds or pearls.

After you have kids, it's more practical things that seem to make it under your tree or into your stocking.

My husband will never live down the year he got me a new kitchen faucet for Christmas (even though I did like it).

This year, I asked for bathroom towels, a $32 bottle of shampoo and a kit for decorating cakes. Sure, if I had millions, I would add a chef, a chauffeur and a couple nannies, and maybe I would request pearls, too.

But I don't, and they'd look quite tacky with jeans and sweatshirts, anyway, and my 2-year-old would find a way to disassemble them and flush them down the toilet or jam them into the humidifier.

Truth be told, there are many things I'd enjoy more than towels, but most are out of the budget, require too much time or are completely unrealistic.

However, just for fun, I'll share a few that might be on my list if the sky was the limit.

* Being deserted on an island for some alone time. Totally deserted—not even Tom Cruise or Brad Pitt could tag along (unless they promised to baby-sit once we got back home.)

* A few nights at Grandhotel Pupp in Prague. Wouldn't it be cool to live it up Queen Latifah-style as she did in the movie, "Last Holiday?"

* Richard Simmons for my personal trainer. He's quite a motivator and much less intimidating than a 20-year-old dressed in Spandex without a spec of cellulite on her body.

* Mary Poppins for a baby-sitter.
* Emeril Lagasse for a personal chef.
* Alice, the Bradys' housekeeper.
* A self-cleaning kitchen. That's right—not a self-cleaning oven, but a self-cleaning kitchen for Alice's days off.
* Tickets to Oprah. I went to a couple tapings of the show about 15 years ago, but tickets aren't quite as easy to come by these days and her topics back then were a little too Jerry Springer-ish.
* A two-seater sports car for the day. Just so I could take a ride in something that you couldn't put a car seat in.
* One of those robot vacuum cleaners.
* A pennant win for the Cubs (I know I'm really entering impossible territory.)
* A night where the kids all get tired and go off to bed on their own without a fuss at 5:30.
* A night at the opera and a dress that doesn't make me look like the fat lady who has to sing before the show can be over.
* A hot tub that is invisible to my kids that I can use after they're in bed and they don't know is there.
* Stylish high-heeled shoes that actually feel like slippers.
* A toilet seat that automatically goes down after being used by someone of the male species.
* A new type of chocolate that works with your body's metabolism to decrease fat cells with each bite.
* Live serenades from George Strait, Alan Jackson, Paul McCartney, Justin Timberlake and Andre Bocelli.
* A maintenance-free garden of daffodils and irises that bloom for eight months out of the year.
* Snow for the six weeks from Thanksgiving to New Year's Day, followed by 70-degree days until June.

The 36 Rules of Motherhood

January 6, 2008

A lot of people forward me silly jokes, chain e-mails, inspirational stories, pithy quotes and wacky videos.

Recently, I got an e-mail titled "36 Rules of Life."

Listed among those life lessons were "Don't worry what people think, they don't do it very often," "If you must choose between two evils, pick the one you're never tried before," "It ain't the jeans that make your butt look fat," and "Never lick a steak knife."

Inspired, I thought I would share "36 Rules of Life for Moms" with you:

1) Breathing during labor is a distraction, not a pain reliever.

2) Breakable Christmas ornaments will last no more than 10.2 seconds in house full of boys.

3) Never get a puppy when you have a newborn.

4) Don't buy purple grape juice; always buy white (unless your home happens to be decorated entirely in purple.)

5) Sleepovers are really stay-upovers. Don't expect to get a wink of sleep.

6) Children are incapable of vomiting in a bucket, bag, toilet or sink; but are very capable of doing it in a place with millions of nooks and crannies.

7) Babies can and will poop all the way up the back of their shirts; that's the real reason Onesies were invented—to be a poop-confiner.

8) If you build mud pies, they will come.

9) One toy + 2 kids = hitting, biting and scratching.

10) 2 toys + 2 kids still = hitting, biting and scratching, because the other toy always is more enticing.

11) Mountain Dew should not be served to anyone until age 12.

12) Wrapping paper and boxes are more interesting than a $100 toy.

13) Teeth fall out when the fairy is short on cash.

14) Kids always seem to feel ill on days when there is an algebra test.

15) Toddlers always fall asleep on a road trip 10 minutes before reaching the destination.

16) Two-year-olds and art museums don't mix well.

17) If a pacifier soothes them, use it.

18) When cooking with kids, always make sure the grown-up cracks the eggs.

19) If they say or do something crude, they probably learned it from their uncle. If they learned it from you, blame it on the uncle.

20) The 102-degree fevers will likely come at 2 a.m. on a Saturday, not 10 a.m. on a Tuesday when the doctor's office is open.

21) Playdates for 1-year-olds are really venting sessions for moms.

22) Ice cream melts faster than a 4-year-old can eat it.

23) Any negative thing you say will promptly be repeated back by a toddler. Any nice thing you want them to say will take 14 times before it sinks in.

24) Teenage years are the terrible twos all over again; only this time they last about six years.

25) Crayons show up darker on walls than on paper.

26) Forty seconds of a child playing in the drivers seat = windshield wipers on, hazard lights on, cruise control set, air conditioning on a full blast, windows down and the radio set to a foreign language station.

27) Children would not eat Brussels sprouts if they were dipped in chocolate, powdered sugar and sprinkles and swimming in a sea of hot fudge and whipped cream.

28) On Mondays, you have to drag them out of bed. On Saturdays, they seem to wake up on their own at 6 a.m.

MOM MOMENTS

29) More syrup gets on the table and chairs than in the mouth.

30) Don't sweat it if they want to eat only raisins, macaroni and cheese and Lucky Charms for a week.

31) In a little one's eyes, child safety locks are a challenge to be conquered, not a deterrent.

32) No one ever died from picking their nose (which, by the way, they're most likely to do during the school Christmas pageant or when you're introducing them to your boss.)

33) A freshly mopped floor attracts muddy feet.

34) Being told to brush their teeth is cause for as much resistance as being told to scrub the toilet.

35) Bank tellers will still accept checks that have Sponge Bob Square Pants drawn on them with a yellow highlighter.

36) They grow up way too quickly.

Parenting inspiration from mom of American Idol contestant

March 2, 2008

I've gotten to be a big "American Idol" fan over the past couple years. I guess it goes back to being 8 or 9 years old singing songs I'd written into a hairbrush. What little kid hasn't dreamed of being a rock star at some point?

I look at those contestants and remember what it felt like to wish I was up on a stage having people listen to my incredible voice. Problem is, I don't have the incredible voice. So, I watch the show, really pulling for these people who do have musical talent and a shot at making a career out of it.

I got a chance to watch part of the first shows of the season and caught the audition of 18-year-old Josiah Leming from Morristown, Tenn. I loved his initial audition. I then watched his auditions in Hollywood, where despite being an early favorite of the judges, he was cut.

Not only was it disappointing because of his obvious talent—he sings, writes his own songs and plays keyboard and guitar—but also because of the story they aired of him living in his car, traveling the country, trying to live his dream of making music.

So, after he was cut, I thought it would be interesting to interview him and write about what he had been doing since being part of the show. It seems I wasn't the only one interested in his story.

MOM MOMENTS

The day I tried reaching him, he appeared on "Ellen" and "Access Hollywood," and had already been visited by a camera crew from MTV. He was out of town doing a radio show when I called.

I talked to his mom and asked about her large family. Josiah, or "Joey," as he is called by family and friends, is the second oldest of nine children (five boys and four girls), ranging in age from 9 to 20.

She gushed about how "gussied up" he looked on "Ellen," thanked me for being a fan and told me she was his "original fan."

Being a mom, I was interested in hearing how she manages such a large family and decided to call her back and maybe get some material for this column on raising kids.

That call ended up being well more than an hour where she talked about her family, her kids' musical talent and living with cancer. She said a lot of interesting and inspiring things, so I thought I'd dedicate a couple columns to the topic.

Sharon Leming, 40, has been battling a rare form of cancer for more than seven years. She was diagnosed in 2000 with ovarian leiomyosarcoma and has endured 16 surgeries, 45 radiation treatments and six cycles of chemotherapy.

According to her Web site, **www.mylifewithcancer.com**, it affects only four people out of a million and there is no cure.

As a mom of a large family, I immediately felt a connection to her, but the further the conversation went on, I learned more about what an amazing person she is.

Sharon married young and had three children. The marriage ended in divorce, but the second time around she found a wonderful man named Don.

Don adopted her two sons and one daughter, and they went on to adopt six children together, all kids they had taken in as foster children. Some of them have special needs and emotional issues from previous homes.

Sharon worked as an Internet programmer until her health deteriorated in 2004. The following year, she lost the use of her legs due to cancer and now spends much of her time in a wheelchair.

When we talked, she had just gotten bad news that an aggressive form of in-patient chemotherapy is her best option. She got that news just before seeing her son's Hollywood Week audition on "American Idol," from the hotel room near the hospital.

She was home the following day to watch him get cut from the show together as a family, including Josiah.

As you're reading this column, she'll be in a hospital room finishing up her round of chemotherapy.

I'll share more on my conversation with Sharon Leming in my next column. You can find out more about Leming by reading her blog at **mylifewithcancer.com**. You can hear Josiah's music at **myspace.com/josiahleming**.

More Mom Moments with Sharon Leming

March 13, 2008

In my last column, I introduced you to Sharon Leming, a mom of nine from Eastern Tennessee that I interviewed after watching her son, Josiah Leming on American Idol. He unfortunately didn't make it to the final 24, but the exposure he got on the show is leading to lots of interest and he will likely be headed for big things, despite being cut from the show.

Being a fan of the show, I enjoyed hearing bits about "Joey" from his mom that you didn't learn on his few minutes of air time. On the show we learned he was a high school drop out, living in his car without his family's knowledge.

He quit high school at 17 to go on the road to pursue music, but has since received his GED. His mom said he was an excellent student who scored way above average on his ACT's—30 on Math and 32 in English. His talent was apparent when the family got a keyboard one Christmas when Josiah was 8 years old.

Sharon had gotten up before the kids to take a bath and suddenly heard "Joy to the World" being played. Josiah had gotten out of bed early to be the first to play it and breezed through learning songs. She said her oldest son is also musically inclined.

After he left school, he hit the road, spending a lot of time in Dallas. His parents didn't know he was living in his car, but learned about it before the show aired. Had she known, she said she probably would have been on the road looking for him. She mentioned how when he went to Atlanta for the initial audition, someone came up to him while sitting in a McDonald's and took his computer from him and ran off.

The computer had all the master songs he'd written on it. While on the road, he worked in restaurants and did day labor, his mom pointed out. "He's a hard worker," she said. "He used to mow every yard in the neighborhood."

He also did school plays and summer productions. "I always had a feeling that some day the world would discover him and then I would have to share him," she said.

There was also another audition not shown on television in which he sang a song he wrote called "Bad News Baby," which the judges liked. And after the cut, his mom said Simon Cowell was nothing but positive and encouraging to Josiah.

And in typical teenage fashion, he packed at the last minute before flying out to tape the Ellen show, discovering on the way to the airport that his flight was leaving an hour earlier than he thought (but he did make it.)

As for mothering her large brood, she said, while the general belief is that children in large families lack attention, she's learned that there is always plenty of company in a large family. "There's always someone that will do something with you," she said. "And we get off and spend time with them in ones or twos."

Leming said she always wanted a dozen kids and likes the craziness and "constant motion" of a large family. She hates that her illness (she has Leiomyosarcoma, a rare form of incurable cancer) has slowed her down.

She explained that the kids in her home go to bed in layers, which allows her to spend quiet time with some of the kids. "The youngest go to bed at 8, then the next set at 9, the older ones in high school at 10 and then the two grown boys never go to sleep." While she's proud of Josiah's musical talent, she said she wants to support her kids, not nudge them. She would have liked to have seen Josiah go off to college, but she also believes there's nothing wrong with taking time off to see the world while you're young.

MOM MOMENTS

Of her nine children, six of them were adopted after taking them in as foster children. For each of them, she said it's taken a long time to integrate them into the family. "They all have histories that make them unique," she said.

Since my last column ran, Sharon has returned from the hospital where she unexpectedly went into a temporary coma. She's now coping with the after effects of the chemo and updating her blog at **mylifewithcancer.com.**

I loved a few of the lines she said during our conversation, including that her parenting theory is "all mysteries eventually solve themselves." If you have some patience and don't panic, sometimes things do seem to fall into place. She also said, "I live today, today and tomorrow, tomorrow." Those are words we all should live by.

Always more to learn about baseball

April 29, 2008

"Teach a boy to throw a baseball and he won't throw a rock."—Ty Cobb

Baseball season is under way, from the Little League fields to the major leagues. It's a pastime that has occupied and entertained young boys for well over a century, giving them a way to expend their energy in a constructive way.

Having a love of history of all kinds, I especially love baseball history. It's a topic that is ever changing as current players join the ranks of the legends and surpass previous records. It's a topic that can be debated on so many levels; which players are the most effective, which team picked up the best rookies in the off-season, which team has the most spirited manager or which ballpark has the most charm. The list goes on and on.

Even those who are not big sports fan can probably look back at their life and recall a significant time in baseball history or name some of the biggest names in the history of the game.

I wrote previously that I had learned about a great-great uncle of mine who played in the major leagues in the early 1900s. It's been so much fun digging up information on him. Originally, all I knew was that he played for St. Louis. Through ebay, I was able to obtain a T206 tobacco card of him from 1909.

I noticed that he died in Danville in 1974 at age 93. I contacted a couple historical societies in central Illinois and was tickled to get an envelope in the mail a couple weeks ago with a newspaper clipping about him from after his death. The article stated that at one time he had tied Ty Cobb's record for fastest run from home plate to first base. That surprised me since in the original material I'd found, he was called "too unreliable" to play every day. During his first year, in 1907, he played only nine games, had seven hits and one RBI.

In doing more research, I learned that his best playing days weren't for the Cardinals, but in the Federal League for the Brooklyn Tip-Tops in 1914 and the Kansas City Packers in 1915. In 1914, he was among the league leaders in slugging percentage and batting average (.324) and had 24 stolen bases. The following year, at age 34, his home runs and RBI numbers were in the top ten of the league.

Unfortunately, his only son, who I don't believe had any children, preceded him in death. It would have been exciting to connect with his descendents.

It really is a wonderful life

April 22, 2008

Most people have seen the Christmas classic "It's a Wonderful Life," in which George Bailey falls on hard times and is convinced that the world would have been better if he'd never been born.

With the help of Clarence, an angel in search of his wings, George gets a glimpse of what the world might have been like had he never existed and sees what a truly wonderful life he has despite the troubles he's facing. He has the wonderful gift of family and friends—possessions that money can't buy—but it takes a nudge from Clarence for him to realize what he has.

A parent is the recipient of the greatest gift there is, a beautiful miracle that they've created that looks to them for guidance and provides unconditional love. However, even with all the joy that children bring, there are days when we overlook how wonderful our lives truly are.

There have been days where breakfast has landed on the floor, homework is colored on by a toddler, the dog has chewed up a shoe, an action figure has been flushed down the toilet and the computer crashes—and it's not even 9 a.m. On days such as this even the calmest of mothers finds herself wishing she was on a deserted island where there are no diapers, no lunches to make, no fights to referee and no messes to clean up.

Once in a while, I find myself thinking, "It can't get any worse!" And at that moment, I kick myself and look at how much worse it really could be.

I think of the mothers that spend birthdays visiting gravesites, rather than celebrating with their children as they've left the world too early due to birth defects, incurable diseases, unexpected accidents or violent crimes.

I think of mothers in countries where monsters torture them and their children, or who live in fear of people who don't think twice about blowing up themselves and taking families along with them.

I think of mothers with children in wheelchairs who will never know what it feels like to run down the sidewalk.

I think of mothers who watch their children dwindle from starvation.

I think of mothers who are so poor they can't provide a Christmas gift or holiday meal for their children.

I think of single mothers who deal with everything I do and much more without help.

I think of mothers who have watched their sons and daughters go off to war and those who did not see them come home alive.

I think of mothers who lost spouses and children on 9/11.

I think of women who want badly to be mothers, but suffer infertility.

I think about mothers who sit in hospital rooms watching their babies fight for their lives.

I think of mothers who can't read a book to their child because they never learned how or because they're blind or deaf.

I think of mothers who have no place to call home and raise their children on the streets, in cars or in shelters.

I think of mothers who have miscarried children they never got the chance to know and who only wish they could clean up a toddler's spill or settle a sibling dispute.

It only takes a moment for the pity party to end and to remember that every moment with my children, good or bad, makes my life wonderful. Is it perfect? No, but it is wonderful—messes, tantrums and all.

Show a little more love and care

April 27, 2008

The "bad ones" just need more love.

I was recently at a store where a child was throwing a tantrum, whipping things out of a cart and screaming. I looked over with sympathy, careful not to stare.

I've been there before—out in public with a child who is misbehaving. And I've felt the stares of others and looks of disapproval, wondering what they're thinking as they're viewing the situation—probably that I'm an awful parent to let my child behave so poorly or that I've done an awful job in rearing him for him to act out in such a way.

Sometimes, I'd wish I had the opportunity to give the old man shooting daggers at me an explanation on how it's an hour past his naptime and he's getting over an ear infection and how he is usually a very sweet child who picks flowers for his mother, loves to snuggle and shares his toys with his brothers.

Instead, I'd try to calm my child down and slip away without any more dirty looks.

When I do witness such situations and my eyes happen to meet that of the mother, I try to smile, somehow letting her know that I'm not judging her, but that I understand. If the smile is returned, I might give her a line of encouragement and set off on my way.

I know how uncomfortable it is when a child doesn't behave the way you'd like and you're glared at like you're a "bad" mom with a "bad" child.

I was talking to my sister recently about it and told her my belief was that kids aren't "bad" and when you encounter one that is exhibiting bad behavior, often the bottom line is that they need more love. My sister agreed.

Sometimes the behavior may come from a feeling of being ignored or not heard. Sometimes it's a test of wills that might be subsided by dealing with them in a loving way.

Sometimes it's simply a matter of timing and they're tired and hungry, but being assuring and patient and offering a distraction can turn things in a different direction.

Parenting is a hard job. And although we sometimes wish we could program them to be perfect angels when we take them out in public, it seems like that's often when they do the most mortifying things.

I'm not trying to excuse bad behavior. Inappropriate behavior has to have consequences.

But the next time you see a child throwing a fit at a park, a playgroup or a mall, try not to look so harshly. Show a little love to the child and parent. It can make a world of difference.

May is a month for mom-memories

May 25, 2008

Each year as May approaches, I feel a knot in my stomach knowing it is the busiest month of the year.

Banquets, picnics, field trips, barbecues, school musicals, parties, parades, Mother's Day, Memorial Day, little league practices and games, graduation parties, retirement parties, showers and weddings are just part of the business.

Throw in two children with birthdays, and it adds to the hectic schedule. This year my oldest also had his confirmation, his class trip and his graduation, and we're in the midst of finishing our back yard, which has been an ongoing project since we had a new garage built last summer.

With all the activity, it can sometimes be difficult to pause and take time to actually enjoy it.

And sometimes you can't fully appreciate something special until you look back on it. I'm typing up this article on my oldest son's birthday with memories of that day still fresh in my mind. Recalling that day makes me happy.

Becoming a mom was overwhelming, but the most incredible experience ever. I'm a planner and tried to plan everything out as I read books (this was 14 years ago when the Internet was in its infancy)—from how labor would go to what kind of baby products we'd use.

MOM MOMENTS

Of course, nothing went as expected. Two weeks past my due date, my 11-hour induced labor ended with forceps and a baby in the neonatal unit due to fluid in his lungs. I was introduced to breastfeeding with a pump, rather than my son. I spent every second I could by his side, and I sobbed when I had to head home without him as he stayed until his 10-day round of antibiotics was complete.

I remember the way he looked snuggled in his bassinet with wires hanging out of his blankets. I remember staring at him for what seemed like forever just waiting to see his eyes open.

I remember slowly waddling down the hospital halls to visit him in the middle of the night. I recall the pink cheeks with the clenched fists pressed up against them and the striped caps that stretched over his little ears.

I remember holding him close and rocking in the chair until I could barely stay awake myself. The early days of motherhood truly have been the happiest days of my life.

My second son also celebrates a birthday this month. He was born five years and five days after his older brother. This experience couldn't have been more different than the first.

I went into labor three weeks early with a week of work left to go. After my water broke, I called a coworker who stopped at the house, and I handed her files and gave her instructions between contractions.

After a few hours and fetal distress, I was wheeled down for an emergency C-section. I was sedated, and he was born about 10 minutes later.

A severe case of jaundice kept him in special care under bilirubin lights where I wasn't able to hold him for several days. As I came out of surgery and was being brought down to my room, a nurse brought him out for just a few seconds for a quick glimpse.

I was amazed at how much he looked like his big brother. Once I was able to hold him, he was an intense cuddler who would only drift off to sleep in my arms, which I attributed to his first few days with insufficient contact, sleeping naked with his eyes covered under the lights.

After he came home, the jaundice worsened and he went to the ER and was admitted to the hospital for a couple more days. It was a rough start for us both, but after that ordeal, the first few weeks were nothing short of heavenly.

Of all the May memories I've stored away over the years, none has been more precious than the dates that I became a mom.

With children comes a zoo

June 8, 2008

When you're a parent, it's hard to get by without having a pet of some kind.

When I was a child, we had all kind of animals over the years. We had dogs, several cats, a couple hamsters, a couple canaries and at one point some chameleons that escaped and we never saw again. We always seemed to have at least one cat, mostly because my younger sister was always bringing home strays and begging to keep them.

When my first son was born we had a Labrador/Terrier mix that my husband got when he was in high school.

He was a great dog and a very spoiled dog. He went everywhere with us. He always got a doggie bag of goodies when we went out to eat. He slept under the covers at the foot of our bed. I bought him bones and toys and wrapped them for him for Christmas and his birthday. We had him until my oldest son was 5 years old.

After we got married, we also took in one of my sister-in-law's cats when she was moving. She was a pretty mellow cat and got along great with the dog and my kids.

I remember that we always used to chase her out of the bassinet and crib when the boys were little because she liked to roll up in the corner and sleep. I was always paranoid that she would smother one of my kids by climbing into the crib when they were napping.

She was fun to have around, but the clumps of hair she left always drove me crazy.

We later got a 120-pound German Shepherd, who was wonderful with the kids. He had been trained as a police K-9, but didn't make the cut. I think they said he wasn't aggressive enough. He was already about 6 years old when we got him, so he was with us for about six years before he made his way to doggie heaven.

Our newest dog we got as a puppy. My 9-year-old really bonded with him when we brought him home a couple years ago. The dog sleeps in the bed with him and when he's gone at school the dog lies on his pillow.

Aside from chewing up an iPod and countless shoes and peeing on my brother's leg every time he sees him, he's been a good dog.

We've had our share of short-lived fish, a bunny and a hamster, which should have been named Houdini. I'll save that story for another time.

Cats, dogs and hamsters I'm used to, but there have been a lot of other animals that my kids have adopted, although often for a short time.

We once had a praying mantis named Cody that we put in a 10-gallon tank. She lived for about a year and it was quite a treat to watch her lay egg sacks and eat live bugs (and even a small snake once.) Every summer we end up with some toads, snakes and caterpillars that we release after a day or two. This spring we had a nest full of baby bunnies living in the yard that my husband built a little shelter for. And last week after a heavy rain, the family scooped up some water full of tadpoles and snails that are now living in a tank on my kitchen counter and being fed frozen lettuce after finding the suggestion on a Web site.

I know I'm not alone. I talk to parents with animals of all kinds as pets all the time, and with summer just beginning, I'm sure we'll be temporarily housing a few more creatures.

Strange to be empty-handed

Sunday, June 22, 2008

For many years, I was the one at parties or outings with a baby in my arms or a toddler on my hip. My last four kids were born in just under six years, so my arms were full continually for a long time.

There were even times I had a kid in each arm.

At a recent lunch date with my son's preschool classmates, I looked around at the other moms with their infants and toddlers in highchairs and strollers.

I felt those pangs of emptiness and also felt sympathy as I watched one of the moms chase her toddler through the restaurant and another as she struggled to keep her little one content during naptime. Been there, done that.

Although there often are moms in the groups that have a few years on me (I'm 35), I suddenly feel like the old lady of the group, often being the only one without a baby in my arms.

My youngest one recently turned 3, but it's been such a drastic change since last summer. I realized recently that this will probably be our first summer in many years that we'll be going places without lugging a double stroller.

If it's going to be a rather long outing, we'll probably take an umbrella stroller for my youngest one, but the days of maneuvering the bulky double-seater are done.

I'm also getting away from bringing the diaper bag along. I finally decided that I needed a bigger purse, since I couldn't fit much in the tiny one I'd been carrying.

Now I have room to stuff a diaper and some miniature wipes in there and by the time they're 3, you don't need much more than that.

Pretty soon, the diapers will also be a thing of the past—and I can't say I'm sad about that one.

The sippy cups also are becoming a relic as they now are used primarily for car trips when spills are most likely to happen. My youngest has mastered using the grown-up cups and utensils.

The binky has been gone for about two years. All the baby clothes and toys have been packed up and sent on to my sister, who is due any day now with her third one, which will be a boy.

At the play date, I got a chance to hold two other little ones as my big boys were busy playing and eating. It brought back the memories of snuggling and rocking, but also of juggling and lugging kids and gear.

As with every stage, it's bittersweet. It's kind of a relief to give my back and arms a rest.

But I can't help feeling a little empty when I'm empty handed.

Siblings can be the best of friends and the worst of enemies

July 6, 2008

I am one of six kids, but grew up with my two younger sisters because my much older siblings were leaving home before I was in kindergarten.

So, it was us three girls—me and my twin sisters, who are two years younger.

The story goes that after I was born, my mom "convinced" my dad that I should have a playmate. They were surprised when I ended up with two playmates. After all, those were the pre-ultrasound and pre-fertility treatment days and the doctor never suspected there was more than one.

Having two kids when you were only expecting one can pose many challenges. My mom had this ideal vision of having two little girls playing dolls together and being the best of friends. Adding another to the mix changed the dynamic entirely.

Having spent some time getting the full attention of my parents and three teen-aged siblings, it was quite a shock to have to share them with not one, but two little sisters. I've heard lots of stories of my jealous streak during that time from my mom.

And while it was true that I now had playmates, it often seemed like I was more of an onlooker to their playtime. If you're a twin or have twins in your family, you know there's a certain bond between them that no one else really "gets." And when you have three kids, there always seems to be someone getting left out.

We had lots of times during childhood when we were all best friends, playing gleefully and peacefully. Other times, we were mortal enemies, pulling hair and kicking one another over something as insignificant as a hair bow. I suppose it happens in every family in some form.

In the past few months, I've seen more than my share of sibling rivalry. While it's happened in spurts over the years, it seems that this year it's gone to the extreme and become a daily occurrence. My five stubborn boys make the catfights I had with my sisters look like a day at the beach.

It can all start with a little action figure that's been sitting untouched in a drawer for weeks. One child pulls it out to start playing with it and then the original owner jumps in to claim it, usually by snatching it from his brother's hands without uttering a word. Next thing I know there's screaming, pushing and hitting. And no one wants to let the other have the last blow, so then I'm jumping in and playing referee to avoid bleeding injuries and broken furniture.

Once they stop and catch their breath, they can be playing together in harmony not 30 seconds later. It's hard to understand. It's something that you'll probably only see among siblings. Witness a bar fight and it's not likely that one guy will slug the other and then play nice and offer to share Legos and fishy crackers with him.

For anyone who has been a sibling and is now a parent to siblings, it just seems to be part of the game. Friend one moment, foe the next. At least I have the comfort of knowing that eventually the petty wrestling matches will come to an end. My sisters and I are now good friends and it's been a long, long time since we pulled each other's pony tail.

I'm a Country Girl Wannabe

July 20, 2008

A couple weeks ago my two oldest boys and I went over to my parent's house for our regular game night, planning to do some rounds of Boggle, Uno and Imaginiff. I had brought a pizza, so my dad put in a movie while we ate and we all got so involved in it, the games never happened.

The movie was called "The Final Season"—a nice family flick that was endearing and sappy, at times bordering on corny, but I liked it nonetheless. It was right up our alley as we are a family full of Cubs fans and the boys have all developed an interest in the great American pastime. And it was right up my alley since it was set in 1990, the year I graduated from high school.

The movie, based on a true story, involves a baseball team from a small high school in rural Iowa, which had an outstanding string of state championships under its belt—something like 20 championships in 23 years, all under the tutelage of a well respected coach.

It was a story of a town that revolved around the game and suddenly, the town was facing the reality that the state board of education would be consolidating schools and baseball would cease to be played at their high school. I loved a scene in the movie where the team went off to play in a state championship game and the entire town shut down because everyone left to go to the game. Things like that don't happen in a suburb of about 30,000.

I found myself fantasizing about moving to that town—Norway, Iowa—with a population of about 600. Part of me loves the idea of living in a place where there are more farm animals than people and the fields seem to go on forever.

Since seeing the movie, the state was overcome by flooding and I've wondered how they've fared (Norway is not far from Cedar Rapids.)

Although I've lived my entire life in the Chicago suburbs, I've always pictured myself one day sitting on the porch of an old farmhouse with kids running about in the open space, even though I probably wouldn't make a very good farm girl.

It's just not my thing—getting dirty, cleaning up after smelly animals, dealing with bugs and all the manual labor that's involved. I'm not an outdoor girl, but a farm sure is nice to look at.

I have a cousin who lives just south of Springfield and we've visited her family on their corn and soybean farm a couple times. Each time I've been there, I really hate to leave. From outside their big house (with the big front porch, complete with a swing,) there are only a couple homes in sight and they're way down the road.

I love gazing out from the yard at night. No streetlights. No blazing security lights. No lights from the expressway in the distance. Just a distant light or two from the neighbor's porch down the road and the glow from the stars and the moon.

It's so nice to look out at an open sky like that without trees and houses and utility poles in the way. No noises or trucks rolling down the pavement of I-80. No loud car radios. No sirens. No dogs barking.

Crickets. Nature. That's what you hear. It feels so serene.

The mornings are equally as pleasant. I'm not a big morning person, but when I'm there, I love to be up early and head outside to see the sun rising against the pale blue sky. There's dew on the grass and the crops. The outdoor cats pounce around ready for their morning meal. An occasional farm truck will roll by on the gravel road in front with a smiling, waving driver. Birds are chirping. Butterflies are dancing.

The couple of days I spend there are such a nice escape to a life so different from my own. A life I love to escape to, but am not quite sure I could adapt to on a permanent basis.

Wising up about summer's end

September 7, 2008

Another summer has come and gone. Well, it's not officially the end of summer yet, but the kids are back to school and the sun's fading in the sky a little earlier, so the writing is on the wall. Fall is creeping up. The calendar is getting jam-packed again with multiple activities written on each day.

Although it's exciting to look ahead at a new school year, I miss summer already. I'm not a real disciplined person and kind of like the freedom of summer. It's fun to spend afternoons in the sun at the pool with the boys and let them play outside until dark. I like not having to rush out the door in the morning to get kids to school, but it's a routine that benefits us all.

I'll miss all the activities of summer and having my kids around. This year is the first time in more than 14 years that I'll have a little span of time where there are no kids at home all day to tend to.

My youngest is now a preschooler three mornings a week. He has been overjoyed about it, so that has made it pretty easy for me. I've also had one entering kindergarten this year, so that was a big step for him, going from being at school three mornings a week to being there all day. And my oldest is a high school freshman this year. It doesn't seem possible, especially when I think that I was a high school freshman when I met my husband. And sandwiched in the middle are a first-grader and a fourth-grader.

A few months back, I wrote a little about a mom I had found so inspiring, Sharon Leming of Morristown, Tenn. Leming has a rare form of cancer and has nine children, six of them adopted. One of her boys, Josiah, had appeared on American Idol last season, but was booted off in the Top 50 (he's since signed a record deal with Warner Bros. records and his CD is due out in the next month or so.)

I've checked in on Leming's blog, **mylifewithcancer.com,** to see updates on her battle with cancer and to read about her everyday life of raising such a large family. A couple lines in a recent posting really hit me—gave me that kick I needed to stop moping about the end of summer and my boys all heading to school and to start happily looking ahead.

She said, "I am sorry that summer is over (for all practical purposes), but it's the natural order of things. One season rolls into another, and we are wise to embrace each one for its own beauty instead of longing for the one that just passed and can never be touched again."

Give other moms support, not criticism

October 19, 2008

You think there's competition in sports. And in academics. And in business. A place you may not expect it to rear its head is in parenting, but mommy competition is all over the place—from the commercials urging you to buy the best baby products to securing a spot in preschool to the debates over breastfeeding, whether or not to work outside the home, to use cloth or disposable diapers, to allowing your child to watch television or eat Happy Meals.

There always seems to be a little whisper in your ear that someone else is parenting better.

It's not necessarily coming from the other moms. It's often our own self-doubt that keeps us feeling as if we're always in competition to do the best for our kids or that there's something we should be doing differently or that someone else's kids have the edge over ours.

And sometimes our own worst critics are other moms who think they know better.

It's always nice when you find other moms you can connect with, but you always have a few with adamant opinions on issues and who won't hesitate to make another mom feel bad about formula feeding or placing their child in day care.

On one hand, we need to realize that one mom's boasting is just a result of pride and not take it personally. On the other hand, there's no quicker way to make an enemy than to insult someone's child or question their parenting style.

Wouldn't it be so nice if we could all get along and not judge other moms? I've been guilty of it myself (mostly early in my parenting career), but I know that we'd all be better off if we could support one another instead of working against each other.

I guess my years of parenting experience have changed my views a bit. While at one time I would have seen a child throwing a tantrum in a store and thought that the mother was doing a poor job of controlling her child, I now feel sympathy. I've been there, done that. I know we all have bad days and our kids do, too. I realize that sometimes a child who appears to be misbehaving may have a medical disorder that causes the behavior and I consider that, rather than jumping to judge the parent.

I have learned that people parent differently and do what works best for them.

That may mean bottle feeding rather than breastfeeding, a family bed rather than a bassinet, private school instead of public school or an array of other choices. It's better to commend other moms for making choices that best suit their family than trying to convince them that they're wrong.

Election provides teaching opportunities for parents

November 16, 2008

Events that happen in everyday life present us with opportunities to teach our children about the world.

The recent election provided many teachable moments to get our children interested in politics, history, geography, world events and civil rights. I'm always amazed at what little sponges they are, soaking up what they hear and see and repeating back what they've learned.

At several area schools, mock elections were held allowing students to cast their votes. It's always interesting to hear the reasons youngsters select the candidates they do. One of my boys said they picked their candidate because they saw a commercial saying that the other would cut Medicare. Another thought that their candidate would do more for education.

A friend of mine, who is white and married to a black man, spent time with her children learning more about Obama's background and showing them the possibilities for multiracial individuals.

I don't watch much television, but when Grandpa baby-sits, he often tunes in to CNN or MSNBC, and his influence was evident when my 3-year-old one day pointed to a newspaper and told me it was a picture of Barack Obama and that he was going to be the next president.

Another day as I was flipping through the channels to find cartoons, he stopped me as a broadcast of a John McCain rally was being televised. When the audience clapped, he told me to clap. When the people stood, he told me to stand. When it was over, he told me, "I like to watch Barack Obama and John McCain."

In the days leading up to the election, we watched a little more television. We watched interviews, press conferences, rallies and biographies of the candidates. My 3-year-old asked questions about who other people were in the videos and why they were doing what they were doing.

While I tried to generate a little interest from my older kids, it was my youngest who was fascinated by everything having to do with the election. On election night, my 3-year-old, suffering from a bout of stomach flu, was curled up on the sofa, glued to the television. He guarded the remote, denying requests from his brothers to switch to Nickelodeon or play a game on the Wii. He drifted off to sleep just before Obama was declared the winner.

Three of his brothers were off to bed early, but knowing the significance of the evening, I invited my oldest to stay up and watch his speech with me, a small consolation for not taking him to see Obama in person in Highland the week before. I'm sure it's something that he'll remember for years to come.

Boys and girls learn differently

December 14, 2008

Boys and girls are different. Duh?

There are the obvious physical differences, but the sexes differ greatly in their behavior and emotional reactions. I'm also a big believer that there are huge gaps in the learning styles of boys and girls and it can affect them in the classroom.

Most schools are geared more towards a female's style of learning.

As a child, I matched the typical learning style of a girl. I was quiet and listened well. I learned well through reading and through visual lessons. I was eager to please teachers and my parents and made a special effort to win their approval.

I usually didn't have a problem with sitting still and staying in my seat. I would be completely content in a silent classroom with a stack of books and worksheets in front of me.

The boys seemed to be poorer students, in general. Many of them were often loud and boisterous. Once in their seats, it usually took a while for them to calm down. They might have to be given verbal directions several times before they would follow them.

They didn't seem as concerned in getting good grades. A lot of them were fidgety, talkative and in and out of their seats, much to the dismay of the female teachers we had until we reached junior high.

I was very fond of my first grade teacher. I can barely recall what she looked like, but I still admire her unusual teaching style. Looking back, it was probably a great environment for the boys. She played a lot of music and encouraged kids to dance and move around and do activities that were interesting to them. She would transition lessons with relaxation and breathing exercises.

Often today a boy's eagerness, excitement and energy can be seen as a downfall or a disability. Sometimes there is a medical explanation for excessively abnormal behavior, but sometimes I think it can be merely a misunderstanding of how boys function and learn.

As a mom of boys, I have seen how they have to be kept busy to keep them out of trouble. They do better when engaged in hand-on activities.

Sometimes when it's to the point that they're verging on uncontrollable, I need just sit them in front of a box of Legos and they are instantly enthralled in building.

In my research of the topic in recent years, I've read about schools that have gone to a same-sex environment, either by creating a single-gender school or by separating boys and girls into different classrooms.

It seems in some cases it's been done as a last resort in poor and/or underperforming schools, but it has proven to be beneficial in curbing violence, enabling students to better concentrate and improving grades and test scores. It's likely a practice that could positively affect schools that aren't on an academic watch list or ridden with violence, as well.

Entertainment choices change once you're a mom

December 28, 2008

I was looking this week through a listing of some of the top in entertainment in 2008, which included downloaded songs (the top two were Low by Flo Rida and Bleeding Love by Leona Lewis), top albums (Alicia Keys, Josh Groban and Lil Wayne made the list) and best selling DVDs, seven of which were family films.

Such lists remind me of how out of touch I am with things.

I guess I'm like a lot of parents out there whose taste in music and movies is tamed down a little once there are little eyes and ears around watching and listening intently to everything they see or hear.

The music I listen to is a little more G-rated than the songs on the top 2008 list that are about licking someone like a lollipop, making love in a club or a girl kissing another girl to see if she liked it.

When it comes to the movies, I don't make it to the theater often to see anything that isn't animated. In the past six months, the only nonanimated movie I saw in a theater was "W," which I went to see at my dad's request. On the DVD list, I saw six of the top 10, all family flicks, except for "I Am Legend."

Of the top grossing movies of the year, four were animated and four others were billed as family movies, although they were PG-13 with some intense action scenes. Two adult-targeted PG-13 movies finished off the list. Only moms would see movies about panda bears doing martial arts or singing chipmunks instead of the "Sex in the City" movie.

It is nice, though, to see that studios are meeting the demand for family movies. Before the computer-animated films started 13 years ago with the release of "Toy Story," there weren't quite as many family films released.

When I looked at the list of top television shows, it was filled with reality shows and crime-related shows.

It makes me miss the sitcoms of my childhood, like the "Cosby Show," "Growing Pains" and "Who's the Boss?" Those were the days when you couldn't watch cartoons 24/7 or watch any movie you wanted at any time of day. So many of the prime-time shows that are on these days aren't exactly family friendly. You can't curl up on the sofa with the kids to watch CSI.

With a few exceptions, like "According to Jim" and the "George Lopez Show," it seems that family comedy sitcoms are a dying breed, allowing more time slots for murder investigation dramas, singing competitions, dance-offs and scavenger hunts through the jungle.

Moms need more than Calgon

March 1, 2009

Moms around my age may remember a television commercial of an exasperated woman declaring, "Calgon, take me away!"

It was an ad for bubble bath, but it's a line many moms have uttered in the midst of chaos, this mom included. Every mother out there has had moments where she just wanted to disappear to relax in silence.

For a long time, my sisters and I have talked about getting away, just the girls. When I was a kid, the girls in my family (my mother, three sisters and two sisters-in-law) took occasional day trips to Long Grove, Ill., a historic village with antique stores and gift shops.

When I was in junior high, my mom went for a getaway with a girlfriend of hers to a bed and breakfast in Chesterton called the Gray Goose Inn. She loved the place and the innkeepers, and our family soon returned.

So finally, my sisters and I picked a date for a girls' getaway.

We decided to go overnight to the Gray Goose Inn. We tossed around the idea of going for a massage, which then turned into a day-long visit to the Waterbird Lakeside Spa at the Indian Oaks Resort. My sister convinced me to get my first pedicure and a 50-minute massage instead of a 30-minute one. We also added manicures and a spa lunch.

It was a getaway we all needed and looked forward to for months: My older sister has a teenage son and recently started working as a hospice volunteer, a result of the months she spent with my brother-in-law as he battled cancer, before she became a widow at age 36. My younger sisters are twins and the one who planned the trip is the mother of a 3-year-old, 2-year-old and 7-month old. My other sister has married and moved recently. She also started a new, demanding job and has had some health problems.

So once we met for lunch to start our weekend, we all sighed with relief.

We spent some time browsing antique shops. It was a Sunday, and we were the only guests, so we made ourselves comfortable in the dining room. We snacked fondue-style, had champagne, played some games, giggled until our bellies hurt and finished the night with a movie.

In the morning we enjoyed fruit parfait, coffee cake and spinach and Swiss quiche before heading off to the spa. I was always reluctant to get a pedicure due to my ugly feet, but it was quite pleasant as was the rest of the day.

Before we left for home, we were already planning our next getaway. While Calgon may be able to take you away temporarily, it's getting away with the good friends you love that makes it so special—and restores sanity.

Parental revenge in the form of a haircut

January 11, 2009

There are many things kids do to make parents shake their heads and wonder what in the world they were thinking. For example, why would a child want to swallow a coin? What would make a kid decide to stick something up his nose? Why would a little one decide to eat a lump of dirt? Why do kids think that a hallway wall makes a great canvas for crayons or markers?

There are a lot of things kids do that don't make a lot of sense.

However, when we think back on our own childhoods, we undoubtedly did a few things that surely made our own parents cringe. Maybe it wasn't eating dirt or coins, but I'm sure there if you really think, something comes to mind.

And for all those senseless things you did, there was probably a time when one of your parents warned you that one day you would have a child that would repeat the senselessness—a sort of parental revenge for all you've put them through. I recall my mother saying on a few occasions, "When you grow up, you're going to have one just like you."

Well, probably my most senseless act occurred when I was around 6. I got the idea to play barber, and my younger sisters were the customers. I proceeded to chop off long ponytails with a pair of scissors. It didn't seem so senseless to me. My long hair had recently been cut after I'd gotten gum stuck in it, and I didn't think it was quite fair that my little sisters still had long hair. So, I chopped away and the only choice my mother had was to cut it short, in what she called a "pixie cut."

I do remember another occasion when I decided to cut my own hair, chopping away at my bangs. Whenever kids decide to cut their own hair, it always seems to be in the most visible of places, right smack in the middle of the forehead.

Well, I got a taste of that parental revenge the other day when my 5-year-old decided to do some cutting of his own. He first found a bottle of gel, which he lathered onto his head and combed it. He proudly exclaimed that he looked "fancy" and that he was ready to go to a wedding.

He returned to the bathroom, where I thought he was simply combing his hair some more, but then he walked out and told me some of his hair fell out. I guess his story was partly true, but he left out the part about how he helped it fall out with a pair of scissors. The evidence was right there—a pair of yellow-handled Fiskars covered with blond strands.

It didn't look too bad at first. It was in a spot where some longer hair combed over it kind of hid the deed. However, my attempt at trying to even it out made it even more obvious—and I'm thinking the summer buzz cut may come a little early this year.

Mothering—In Any Generation—Isn't Easy

April 26, 2009

One recent e-mail from **babycenter.com** caught my interest. It included results of a survey of 2,400 moms with comments on everything from their dislike of technology to the guilt they endure today.

The gist of the article compared who had it easiest—us or the moms of previous generations. Fifty-three percent of moms surveyed said their mom had easier, and 47 percent said their grandmothers had it easier.

My first thought was, "How on earth can we say we have it harder with all the conveniences we have that the previous generations didn't?"

We have microwaves, dishwashers, washing machines, telephones, televisions, GPS devices, fast food establishments, online shopping, digital cameras, DVD players, baby monitors, plastic sippy cups, disposable diapers. Many moms before us lacked most of these luxuries. All of these are things that make our lives easier, right?

Some moms thought the trade-off for such conveniences were more worries and stress, a lack of friendliness in neighborhoods, too many choices, competition among parents and a heightened awareness of danger.

I hesitate to say any generation had it easier than another in rearing children. Years ago, a mother didn't worry about AIDS, but her children might have died of pertussis or rubella or been crippled by polio, which we now have vaccines for.

Earlier moms may have had milk delivered to their homes but didn't have a 24-hour convenience store to run to in a pinch. Many of them wouldn't have had an automobile to get there if there was one.

Moms of long ago didn't have credit or debit cards to use on a whim. However, a mom-and-pop establishment might have accepted an I.O.U. or extended an interest-free line of credit just out of kindness.

A major point of comparison is the danger issue. Are there really so many more dangers today, or do we just know more about them? Moms of other generations had lead in water and paint in toys, but they didn't know it. There were sex offenders on the loose, but they didn't have an Internet database to see how many were in their neighborhood.

I think moms of earlier generations felt more secure about letting their children explore the world outside their home. The kids walked to school. They gathered in fields to play sports or wandered down to fishing holes. They might have had a job delivering papers, shining shoes or stocking shelves before they became teens. From other adults and other children, they learned life lessons.

Today's generation is more paranoid. Children are always in sight and supervised. Instead of walking two miles to school, we drive them a few blocks.

Labor laws and safety measures prevent them from doing most jobs until they're almost done with high school. And we'd never dream of letting a 7-year-old head out by himself to a desolate pond to catch some fish. Kids don't have the opportunity to run around and play in their neighborhoods.

I'd agree times were simpler for earlier moms, but not necessarily easier. What do you think?

Palin encourages abstinence among teens

May 10, 2009

As I tuned it to bits and pieces of television this week, I caught part of an interview with Bristol Palin on a morning show. I didn't see her entire appearance, but decided to look up an earlier interview, yet after she became a mother, where she said that abstinence is the best course for teens to follow, but it's not realistic.

I know she's getting a lot of criticism. Yes, she got pregnant as an unwed teen and yes, she is now a mother—all the result of a bad decision.

Let's face it. Teens make mistakes and bad decisions. Some drink, do drugs, steal, commit violent crimes. Sometimes they are doozies with harsh consequences. The consequence of the error she and her boyfriend made was having a baby long before they had planned. Even so, she's called her son a "blessing" and said that she doesn't regret having him, but would have liked to have had him 10 years later.

According to **childtrendsdata.com**, about one-third of teens report being sexually active. When broken down by grade, it shows that about half of all high school seniors are sexually active.

There's no denying that abstinence is best for teens. It prevents unwanted pregnancy, sexually transmitted diseases and emotional distress that can result from engaging in a sexual relationship.

However, expecting all teens to practice abstinence is, as Palin said, unrealistic. Adults can preach to teens about the risks, but sometimes it still happens, even when you're talking about an honor student, a star athlete or a doted-on daddy's girl. No matter how good of a head the teen has on her or his shoulders, it's hard to rationalize with a teenager in love with raging hormones.

On the flip side, you have girls who don't have a father figure in their lives or who have been abused early in their lives and who crave the attention they can get, even if it involves unprotected sex. Every case is different and teens have sex for different reasons. I'm all for encouraging abstinence, but also think there needs to be education about safe sex.

There have also been changes in how teen pregnancies are handled from generations ago, as well. In, say the 1950s, a pregnant 17-year-old would have likely been forced to marry quickly or forced to give a child up for a closed adoption that left no opportunity for future contact. There are now more options should pregnancy occur and there are more methods of birth control that are easily available.

Rather than continue to heap on the criticism, I think maybe we all need to lay off Palin a bit. Perhaps she can make a difference by sharing her experience and not glorifying teen pregnancy. She's acknowledging the joy of motherhood, but also the hard work and sacrifices that come along with it. She's incredibly fortunate to have family support. And most importantly, she's expressing that she wishes she would have waited.

We all feel loss as show business mourns three greats

June 28, 2009

We lost three icons in the entertainment business this past week. All three hold a special place in my heart, as I know they do in many of my generation. Ed McMahon had that grandfatherly charm and an unmistakable voice that greeted viewers on the television screen for late night comedy. In my house, the start of the nightly 10 p.m. news was always the signal for bedtime.

Sometimes I'd sneak back down the stairs and listen to the news waiting for that familiar call of "Heeerrreee's Johnny!" Occasionally, I'd convince my parents to let me stay up late if it was a Friday or a summer night with no school the next day and we'd watch the Johnny Carson show together. Even if it was actually called "The Tonight Show," I always knew it was Johnny who was the star and thought of it as the Johnny Carson show. Even as great as Johnny was, it was the combination of Carson and McMahon who made the show amusing. McMahon was the often quiet sidekick, but the interaction between the two made it so hilarious. I recall scenes where one would laugh and then the other couldn't stop and their laughter was just contagious.

Farah Fawcett was the ultimate beauty from my childhood. I think every female on the planet wanted those flowing feathered locks at that time. I recall watching the show with my family and in a silly way, it was a groundbreaking show. Not many females on television had such empowering roles. Watching Farrah and the girls investigate cases and bring down the bad guys gave little girls hope that they could be anything they wanted to be when they grew up.

The loss of Michael Jackson is probably felt the greatest in our region, not only because he was the King of Pop, but because we seem to feel some ownership over him since he grew up in Gary and it's where his career began.

Those of his generation may have seen some of his early performances in the area with the Jackson 5 and grew up listening to his young voice and followed his career over the years. I remember spending many summer days in my youth carrying a boom box with a cassette tape of Michael Jackson songs. For me, as a 10-year-old girl, there was nothing more monumental in the universe in 1982 than the debut of the "Thriller" video. With the costumes, the dancing and the voice-over by Vincent Price, it was both terrifying and enthralling.

Unfortunately, today's youths probably know Jackson more from cracks by comedians, parodies and a tarnished reputation than his musical accomplishments. While the latter part of his life was full of allegations and tales of strange way of life, there's no denying that his early life was one of superior talent and artistry. He'll be missed everywhere, especially in the neighborhood he came from.

Mourning an Incredible Mom

July 5, 2009

On nights spent up late, when the house was quiet and the kids all asleep, the last thing I would do before turning in was to go to MYLIFEWITHCANCER.COM and see if there was a new blog entry.

The blogger was Sharon Lemming, a lady I have never met face to face, but have thought about often since we first talked. If you are a regular reader of this column, you may remember me writing some columns about her last year.

When I first "met" her via telephone, it was right after her son, Josiah, appeared on "American Idol." Surprisingly, he was not selected to advance from the early rounds though he seemed to be a favorite of the judges. After they aired the show where he was cut, I tried contacting him for an interview. Instead, I reached his mother, who told me he was taping "The Ellen DeGeneres Show" in California.

Even over the phone she seemed like one of those friendly, inviting, hospitable people who makes strangers into instant friends. For some reason, that short phone inquiry resulted in a conversation that lasted about an hour and a half. She shared all kinds of stories about her son that he probably would have preferred that she did not.

She also talked about her battle with cancer and directed me to her blog.

We exchanged a few e-mails after that. Mostly, I kept reading her blog to find out how she was doing.

I knew I'd found a special individual and ended up writing about her in four different columns. I was amazed at how Lemming and her husband, after having three children, went on to adopt six more children who needed homes. They all came to live with the family as foster children and became permanent residents.

Her outlook on life was amazing. Reading poetry posted on her blog, you can see where her sons got their songwriting talent.

On June 16, Sharon Lemming lost her nine-year battle with Leiomyosarcoma, a rare form of incurable cancer.

My heart breaks for the husband, children and extended family that she left behind. Losing a parent is devastating no matter what age the children are. In this case, they range from about 10 to 21.

So, as the world is mourning the loss of the celebrities who have died over the past couple weeks, I'm remembering someone who also touched the world and leaves an empty space for those who knew her. Even if they only knew her through a blog.

Birthdays bring back memories

August 2, 2009

My fourth son just turned 6 years old.

On his birthday, I had to do some shopping and invited him along on a trip to Kmart. It is always nice spending one-on-one time with each of the boys. While there, I told him he could pick out a toy since it was his birthday.

I was expecting Legos or an action figure. Nope. He wanted the SpongeBob skateboard.

I tried to sway him toward something a little less dangerous, but he was set on the skateboard. I explained that he'd have to wear a helmet and knee and elbow pads and he agreed.

When we got home, he tried it out and wiped out within 15 minutes. I'm hoping there's not an ER visit in my future as a result of his birthday pick.

At birthday time, you revisit the day that little bundle arrived. I was due July 23 and was having contractions after a morning visit to my obstetrician. While I was trying to nap on the sofa, the door bell rang. It was a delivery of my second book, set to be out in stores that week. I was so excited, but didn't even open it to look inside. Within a couple hours, I was on my way to the hospital.

We knew we were having another boy and I loved the name Conner. My husband wasn't so keen on it because we already had two boys with "C" names. So, the alternates were Brandon (his choice) and

Justin (mine.) All three of the other boys were named before they were born, although I did have a last-minute change on my second one's middle name.

When our fourth was born, we were still unsure what to call him. We pondered for a couple days and figured we needed to decide.

Neither my husband nor I had a strong preference, so we decided to let our oldest son, then 9, choose the name. When I was pregnant with my second son and he was 4 years old, he was adamant about naming his brother Elwood Butter. He was crushed that we weren't as enthusiastic as he was about his choice.

This time we gave him three choices: Brandon, Conner or Justin. He settled on Brandon and Conner seemed a good fit as a middle name.

Brandon Conner was the largest of my boys at 8 pounds, 5 ounces, but the easiest of my labors. He didn't quite make it in on his due date and waited until the wee hours of the morning to arrive.

It's unbelievable that it's been six years. My, how time flies!

The one who dies with the most toys wins

August 23, 2009

The one who dies with the most toys wins.
I've heard that phrase many times and a few of those times those words were spoken by Don Parker, a dear family friend for the past two decades.

Those were the first words to pop into my mind when I heard that Don had passed away earlier this month.

Don, who is formerly of Glenwood, has been a friend of my mom and dad since I was a teenager. He was at my wedding and has seen my kids growing up. One year I recall meeting him at his company in Chicago Heights when my oldest was a toddler and he was taking an old Army truck that he had and driving it in a local parade. Don let us ride along and my son was thrilled. Also on the float were members and kids and grandkids of the Lions Club or a similar service organization. Don always loved having the opportunity to take his truck for a ride and was great about helping out other groups in the process.

My husband and Don got to be good friends and bonded due to their common interests of machines, vehicles, engines, toys and the outdoors. A few years back Don built a house on some land he had in southwest Michigan and the house is surrounded by dozens of acres. He built a huge pole barn and started his collection of what he called "big boy toys." Each time we'd go up for a visit, he'd show us the new items he'd picked up at a recent auction. His "toys" ranged from military trucks to tractors to even a school bus, which he used as a playhouse for one of his dogs. He always seemed to have a herd of Weimaraners strolling around the property.

I remember him once describing his vision of a "Big Boy Theme Park" where grown men would come to play. Instead of a theme park that featured amusement rides, his theme park would be like a construction site and the rides would be real bulldozers, trucks and tractors. I thought it was a brilliant idea. I could see lots of guys forking out money to spend a day playing with full-size versions of the toys they played with as boys.

Don was always happy to see us on our visits and I was greeted with one of his big bear hugs. He was a tall and sturdy guy and you seemed to be swallowed in his embrace.

My husband would often visit alone or with a couple of the older boys and they'd explore the property on ATV's. It seemed to be his manly escape from the rest of the world. But whenever we'd head up there, Don always seemed to have something planned later in the day. He was quite active—always running off for dinner, a concert, billiards or some other activity.

On our most recent visit in mid-June, Don wasn't feeling well after being diagnosed with Lyme Disease. He was full of vigor in conversation, but a bit thinner and weaker than I was used to seeing him. His collection had also expanded since our last visit and the toys he cherished were at every turn. Even as I looked around that day, his voice echoed through my mind. "The one that dies with the most toys wins."

Well, Don, you've won, but we've lost a great friend.

Silence of back-to-school time is bittersweet

August 30, 2009

The first day of school is usually harder on Mom than it is on the kids. Here they are heading off with all this cool new gear to a new environment to make new friends. We mothers then get a few hours of peace and quiet, but that bit of newfound silence is bittersweet.

The days of summer still linger, but there are no kids there to take to the park or the pool. No one to pour Kool-Aid for or hand Popsicles to. No one to take a walk with or read a book to. No one to play catch or a board game with. No one to tag along to the grocery store. The absence of the noise, motion and quarrelling between siblings can be refreshing on one hand, lonely on the other.

This will be my last year of having a little one around during the day. Last year he went off to preschool for three half-days and he'll do the same this year. We're both easing into the school situation with him next year heading off to school full-time.

This school year, the kids are returning gradually—one during the third week of August, another the following week and the other three not starting until tomorrow.

I listen to other moms that have been there tell me that next year when they are all in school, I'll be relieved to have the long span of quiet time and will welcome the freedom that comes with it. I know it will be true—to some extent. I know I'll have plenty to do. There are never enough hours in the day. And I suspect I'll pile on the work to occupy myself so I don't notice that no one's asking for a snack and I don't hear Dora coming from the television screen.

For now, I'll savor this last year of snuggling in the afternoon watching cartoons, making trips to the library, running errands together and meeting other youngsters for play dates. Even if he can be loud and moody and messy, I love hanging out with my 4-year-old and I know that next year I'll miss our day time fun terribly.

10 THINGS I'VE LEARNED FROM BOYS

September 13, 2009

    It's always a great day when you learn something new. Sometimes it's something you hear from a friend or acquaintance. Sometimes you stumble across something on the Internet. Often a newspaper or magazine article informs you of something you didn't know. And, in parenting, you always learn new things. I do have two big brothers, but admit I didn't know much about boys until I had them. And with five of them, I'm getting to know the other gender better all the time.

    Here's a few of the things I've come to know in my 15 years of mothering males.

* Boys are loud and destructive.
* Boys add motor noises to just about anything.
* Boys give the most wonderful, tight hugs.
* Toads don't like being squeezed.
* The more they bleed after an injury, the cooler it is.
* Boys like mud.
* Boys don't like to clean up mud.
* Some boys actually like to cook.
* They CAN be trained to put down a toilet seat.
* If you spray a half bottle of baby powder into the air, you'll set off the smoke detector.

Real men (and boys) cook

September 27, 2009

There once was a time when men didn't have a place in the kitchen. Cooking was considered woman's work and the kitchen was expected to be the female's domain.

Isn't it nice that those days are over?

That shift in thinking is partly due to the presence of cooking shows featuring top-notch chefs like Emeril Lagasse and others. With the birth of the Food Network, it was suddenly acceptable for a guy to not only make a meaty meal of brats soaked in beer or ribs slathered in a spicy finger-lickin' sauce that was prepared on a behemoth-sized grill, but also to whip up a quiche, prepare a perfect crepe or labor over the stove sautéing veal in wine sauce.

I can't say I married one of those guys, but my husband is a great breakfast cook. He makes one mean omelet—usually with lots of veggies and cheese oozing out of the sides. Weekend breakfasts are usually left to him.

In my days before motherhood, I envisioned myself in the kitchen with my little girls baking cakes and cookies, but after I had my first son, I realized that boys can enjoy cooking just as much. He always loved helping me with recipes by cracking eggs, stirring and scooping. When he was about 4 or 5 years old, he would often create "recipes." I'd just sit back and humor him, assuring him that his egg, orange juice and oregano pudding would taste wonderful.

His hobby was short lived and now that he's 15, he shows little interested in making meals unless he's begged to throw some hamburgers or chicken on the grill. With my 10-year-old, however, it's a different story. A couple years ago I ordered some kid-sized aprons for the preschool class and put each child's name on them after the title of "chef." I had extras, so I also made them for my kids. About once a week, he'll pull out his apron and request a cooking lesson.

I'm the daughter of a wonderful cook, but I don't remember spending much time in the kitchen actually cooking or learning how to make the dishes from my mom.

We girls tended to make a mess of the kitchen, so she usually put us to work at the dining room table snapping green beans, buttering toast or peeling eggs.

Cooking is a messy job, but I try to put that out of my mind and enjoy the time spent together in the kitchen with my boys.

In the past couple weeks, my 10-year-old has prepared—with supervision, but little or no assistance—hamburgers, hot dogs and bratwurst on the grill, sloppy Joes and beans, a pork tenderloin with rice and asparagus, sausage and noodles, cinnamon rolls, pancakes, homemade soup, cookies and a no-bake cheesecake. It's quite refreshing to eat a meal I didn't have to cook. Then to top it off, his dinners usually are accompanied by a tablecloth, goblets, candles and fresh flowers on the table.

Yesterday, my 6-year-old decided he wanted to get in on the action when I told him I was making chili. He carefully browned the meat, added spices, opened cans, diced tomatoes and stirred and the results were delicious. I'm glad they're having so much fun cooking—and I could definitely get used to this.

Common interests helps communication with teens

October 11, 2009

As kids turn in to teens, it can be hard to find things that you have in common. I've been lucky in that my 15-year-old son and I share a love of sports, theater, movies and music. Our common interests lead us to doing a lot of things together—attending baseball games together and watching them on television, going to plays and listening to music and seeing it performed live.

As for the music, I can partially credit the video game phenomenon for that bond. It was through Guitar Hero that he came to know many of the bands that I listened to as a preteen and teenager. Like me, he likes different types of music, but I love it that he appreciates the tunes that defined my youth. When he started taking guitar lessons, he wasn't interested much in learning current hits. He was much more about learning to play Queen, Guns N' Roses or Bon Jovi's early hits.

He's not the only teen who has learned to love bands that have been around since long before he was born. A new generation of fans of AC/DC, Kiss, Aerosmith, Def Leppard and other bands of the 70s and 80s have emerged, worshiping rockers that are old enough to be their grandparents.

This past summer definitely saw a renewed interest in the music of my generation. First, following the death of Michael Jackson, his hits were played repeatedly introducing his music to kids who entered the world long after the introduction of "Beat It" and "Billie Jean." The music of Michael Jackson, Prince, Madonna and many others hold for me childhood memories of a time before adult responsibilities.

Next came the death of John Hughes, an immense talent who through movies seemed to reach inside each of us as youths and expressed our fears and insecurities. Some of the great music hits of the time came also from the soundtracks of Hughes' movies.

I recently went to see the "Footloose" musical at the Theatre at the Center in Munster. My son came along for the production. It was another blast from the past for me. I remember going to see the movie at our local theater when I was about 11 years old and you could watch a show for $1. The love song, "Almost Paradise," was the theme of my junior high dance.

When it comes to music, my parents and I couldn't have been farther apart in taste when I was his age. My father, an avid listener of classical music, wouldn't let us watch MTV with the sound on. He hated rock music—always has and still does. He refers to it as "noise."

My mom always listened to country music and although I wasn't so keen on it back when it wasn't cool, I love country music now and probably listen to it more than any other type of music. We always teased her for her taste in twangy tunes.

My son and I also have a common love of baseball and he now knows way more about the game and the players than I do. He was lucky enough to win a contest to be a celebrity bat kid at a Cubs game and last weekend I had the thrill of watching him sit in the dugout before the game as major league players stood inches away. I shared in his excitement and remembered what it was like being a fan at his age.

Once you've got a teen in the house, there's often less communication and less time spent together and you're grasping at anything you can just to get them to expel a full sentence from their lips. It seems like yesterday that I was watching my son take his first steps and now suddenly he's a young adult. And I'm grateful for the time we have together sharing our common interests.

The Complications of Simple Technology

November 8, 2009

    I'm sitting at my computer and I glance at the clock. It's been a half-hour since I told my 15-year-old son to unload the dishwasher. I know how to get his attention. I open a chat screen and type "Hellooo—are you going to unload the dishes?" In 10 seconds, I get back "yes" and he puts down the laptop and marches into the kitchen.
    Old folk like me are continually amazed at the wonders of technology. A nagging request goes unanswered, but an instant message, chat request or text message can do the trick.
    It makes me think back and wonder how families functioned in the days when I was younger. So, allow me to reminisce for a few moments.
    Cell phones weren't around until I was out of high school and at that time, they weren't portable. You could use them only in cars connected to the cigarette lighter. They were a mammoth size and weighed as much as a newborn.
    So, how did we communicate? The kicker is that we probably communicated a lot more back then—face to face and verbally, anyway. The Internet was probably around when I was in high school, but I didn't discover it for a few more years. No one had e-mail addresses and there weren't chat rooms. All of our communication was by (cue the gasps) land-line phone with a long cord that got all twisted up, by having in-person conversations or by passing folded notes during

class or in the hallways that were often intercepted by someone they weren't intended for.

Worse yet, go back a few more years to my parents' childhood days and things were much more dismal. Before televisions were in every household, you resorted to listening to the radio—or even reading—to keep you entertained. Homes only had one of something—one radio (or black and white television if you were lucky), one rotary phone, one automobile.

Here we are today where nearly every home has multiple items. My house has four computers, four televisions, three land-line phones (two of them cordless), three cell phones, two automobiles, five gaming systems and three hand-held game systems. That's just way too much technology for me, not to mention the fact that those electronics are outdated within a year.

Somehow all these items that were meant to make life easier and simplify things have done just the opposite. In the old days, things were actually simple. You wrote someone a letter, you picked up the phone in your kitchen and dialed, you used cash to instead of debit cards—and when you wanted your child to do the dishes you called his name instead of sending him a text message.

There are many blessings to count this year

November 22, 2009

About this time each year, I, along with many others, take time to reflect on all the blessings in my life and remember all that I have to be thankful for.

Not only is it about being grateful for what you have, but seeing that silver lining even on a cloudy day and recognizing that even tough situations can bring some good.

In looking around at my life and my surroundings, I see so many things to be appreciated. Here are a few thoughts:

On a recent chilly, rainy and very windy day I was stopped at a red light and saw an American flag blowing in the wind. Although the weather was a bit depressing, the sight of that flag perfectly extended due to those high winds brightened my day. The American flag is such a beautiful sight and I'm grateful to live in this country.

One day my 6-year-old happened to have a day off school on a day when his 4-year-old brother had school. The preschool teacher had invited him to come spend some time in his old classroom, so he and I visited for the morning. Although the two quarrel more often than they get along, they seemed to be great buddies that morning. They played together in the classroom and on the playground and walked down the hall with their arms around each other. I was reminded of how special it is to have siblings and how that bond will be there throughout their lifetimes.

MOM MOMENTS

I attended a Veteran's Day memorial service that was very touching. The speakers and the music were powerful, but the end was what really got me. Every veteran there joined on the steps of the memorial. There were individuals of all age who had served at different times—some in peace time, some at war. It was such a reminder of how much our freedom and our way of life depends on them and others like them. I thought about those in my own family, which includes two uncles who served in the Korean War, an uncle who was part of the Battle of the Bulge during World War II and a grandfather who served during World War I. My mother lost a cousin in Korea and another during World War II. Both my father and father-in-law are veterans, as is my brother. I am thankful for all those who have served and all those that are away from their families now serving for our country.

My boys often play rough and tackle each other. Our home is a rowdy place to grow up. One day as they were wrestling playfully, I just stopped to think about how lucky am I that they're healthy enough to do so. I've been fortunate that our trips to the doctor have been minimal and routine for the most part. I know others with little ones that face serious health issues each day, have chronic and potentially fatal illnesses and have had numerous surgeries. To have had five sons who are healthy and strong is such a blessing.

Having lost all my grandparents by age 10, (one died before I was born and another when I was a toddler) I feel so lucky that my children have gotten to know their grandparents. Both my parents and my in-laws have been married for more than 45 years and they all live close by. I love the interaction they have together, whether it's planting a garden with one grandpa or a trip to McDonald's with the other.

And, I'm thankful that I've been able write columns like this one for a decade now and for all those who stop me in the grocery store to let me know they read an article or e-mail me with comments. I love hearing from readers.

Send holiday greetings to troops with a handprint

December 6, 2009

As we head into the season of giving, we can get carried away with elaborate presents or have feelings of inadequacy fearing our gifts won't measure up. We sometimes overlook that it's not giving of material things, but of one's self in the form of friendship, thought and care that really defines the season.

With that in mind, why not take a few moments with your children in the next few days to send a card and some kind thoughts to someone in our military who won't be home celebrating with their family this Christmas.

If you don't know anyone currently serving in the military, you can visit **ANYSOLDIER.COM** to find more than 2,000 contacts.

I'll share a poem I wrote a couple years ago for my son's preschool class to send in packages to troops in Iraq. Each child painted their hand and put a handprint beside the poem.

For the past four years, my oldest son and I have been involved in a project where we mail care packages to soldiers. We place one of these poems and handprints in each package and several times we've gotten thank you notes stating that the candy, snacks, shampoo, magazines, DVDs and other goodies were appreciated, but it was that simple poem and handprint that meant the most.

So, feel free to print the poem and have your child, grandchild, nephew or neighbor decorate it. Giving such a small thing will mean a lot to our servicemen and women.

MOM MOMENTS

Dear soldier:

We know it must be hard
To be so far away
Serving your country
Each and every day

We pray for your safety
And that you'll soon be home
Until you make it back
Know you're not alone

I'm sending you a hand to hold
To help you make it through
Times when you feel sad or alone
Remember we're proud of you

And we say THANK YOU
To you for all that you do

Getting two front teeth for Christmas

December 20, 2009

It seems like forever since I had an empty space in my mouth where a tooth once was. It has been a long time (second grade, I believe) but I can still remember how awkward it felt to slide my tongue around and feel nothing.

I remember how uncomfortable it was as it hung by a thread. Excited to get it out of my mouth, more for the financial reward it brought than the relief of the dangling fang, I tugged and helped it along. It was close to Christmas and when I'd hear the song "All I Want for Christmas is My Two Front Teeth," I'd proudly sing along, pleased with the slight mispronunciation that resulted from that missing tooth.

It wasn't a real complicated part of childhood. A tooth fell out. A new one grew in its place. But it was pretty significant to me. Most of my classmates had already lost their teeth. It seemed like I was lagging behind and it was a bit of a blow to my confidence and self-esteem being one of the few kids left with a mouth full of pearly white baby teeth.

Once those front teeth were missing, I was noticed more, but it didn't seem like it was in a good way. Again, most of the other kids were beyond that stage and when my grin exposed my gums or a gob of spit escaped when I spoke, other kids were there to point out the flaw.

MOM MOMENTS

However, knowing a shiny quarter would be waiting in the pocket of the little brown and blue pillow my mother had made caused enough elation to overshadow the highlighting of my dental imperfection. Besides, it was one of the first signs that adulthood was down the road and that I was growing up—something you're so eager to do at age 7 or 8. Losing the first tooth is a huge experience for a kid.

I should point out that—ironically—a shiny quarter was the exact amount that a candy bar sold for in those days and if I added a penny to it for the sales tax, a gooey Snickers bar was mine. As a sparkling new tooth was coming in, I was coating it with sugar and goo thanks to that pay-off I got for the old tooth.

Here we are just days before Christmas and my second-grader is in the same boat. A few weeks ago he lost his first tooth in the top center, followed by its neighbor a couple weeks later. His smile has since been one of swollen pink gums.

He squealed with delight as he found a crisp $5 bill under his pillow after each exchange with the Tooth Fairy (apparently there's been quite a spike in inflation since I was a child.)

It actually seems like it's been quite a while that I've been staring at a blank spot in his mouth. I'm sure it seems like forever to him. But his grown up teeth will be there soon enough, throwing a shocking reminder towards me that my little guy is heading farther down that road to grown-up land. Moments like that are always bittersweet for moms.

The thrill seems to be wearing off for him. He's been increasingly irritated with how it has changed his appearance and the way he talks and that it prevents him from enjoying an apple. We're planning a visit in the next couple days to see Mr. Claus and I'm curious to see if a new set of choppers makes it on to that wish list.

ONE MOM IN FAVOR OF LATER SCHOOL START DATE BY '12

January 31, 2010

It's winter, but I'm thinking summer—and a longer one.

I caught a bit of news last week that I was happy to see. It was the approval by the Indiana Senate Education Committee of the proposal of Senate Bill 150. A positive vote by the Senate will mean that elementary and high school students in Indiana won't head back from their summer breaks prior to Labor Day starting with the 2012-13 school year.

I've heard comments from opponents of such mandates that this change would affect school test scores and hinder academic achievement. However, I see a few advantages that would come with this new schedule.

An obvious effect of the legislation would be an extended summer, which allows for a little more family time. I cherish those long summer days spent at the pool and the park and would love to have a few more of them to enjoy with my children.

While we can't predict what the weather will be like from year to year, July and August are typically the warmest months in our area, with the average high temperature in Chicago being 84 degrees in July and 83 degrees in August. The average high in June is 80.

It may seem like a slight difference, but spending a few more days in the classroom in early June often means cooler outdoor and indoor temperatures. For schools that are fully air-conditioned, the temperatures aren't an issue, but many schools in the area are without air conditioning. The schools I attended didn't have air conditioning and I can recall how miserable it felt to be in a sweltering room and how difficult it was to concentrate on school work in those conditions.

In a typical year when it starts to cool off a bit in early September, students are better able to focus on work without the distraction of extreme temperatures.

Starting the school year after Labor Day would mirror Indiana's neighbor to the north. Michigan, along with Minnesota and Virginia, prohibit schools from starting before Labor Day. In Wisconsin, Iowa and North Carolina, schools cannot begin prior to Sept. 1. I'm hoping Illinois will also soon follow suit. Chicago schools traditionally start after Labor Day, but throughout the rest of the state, start dates vary from one school district to another.

Aside from the convenience, the weather and the extension of a relaxing summer, there is an economic impact, as well. The tourism and hospitality industries have suffered quite a blow in the past decade with a decrease in travel following Sept. 11, then the spike in gas prices that halted more vacations and now the recent downturn in the economy.

A couple of years ago, we pushed back our family vacation so not to interfere with Little League season, summer enrichment classes, swimming lessons and July Fourth celebrations. I arranged a trip through Indiana and Kentucky during the second week in August. We were surprised to find upon arrival in Kentucky that school was already back in session. That meant that many of the tourist spots we planned to visit were closed for the season or had limited hours. Because kids in both Kentucky and Tennessee were in school, those families had ceased traveling and because the bulk of the work force at water parks and theme parks are high schoolers, the attractions were left without a staff. It was disappointing for us, but it was disheartening to see how the school starting date affected the local economy, particularly the family-owned businesses that were already struggling.

Believe me, I am all for educating kids, but I'm just not sure it's worth the cost. I don't understand the value in sending kids back so soon. By starting after Labor Day, you're not sacrificing the number of days kids are in school, just altering specifically when they are there. Are they going to memorize historical facts or catch on to algebra easier on Aug. 19 than on Sept. 9? I'm thinking it may be the reverse. But that's just one mom's opinion.

It really is the thought that counts, not the gift

February 14, 2010

Ah, it's Valentine's Day.

I can't help but reflect on some of the past Valentine's Days. We always hear the phrase "It's the thought that counts," and as the years go on, it really rings true. It's not so much the gifts that you recall, but the thought or effort that went into them.

Way back in junior high when I was about 12 years old, I remember walking through the neighborhood delivering newspapers after school. I'm not completely certain, but I believe it was The Times (at that time everyone called it the Hammond Times) that I was throwing on front porches. The papers were delivered in the afternoons on weekdays. Anyway, I was on my route and it was cold and snowy and getting dark. I was pretty tired and hurrying to finish and get home and as I came around a corner, waiting there was this boy that I really liked.

He knew I'd be delivering papers and went out to find me to deliver a box of candy. It made my day.

Fast forward a few years. My husband and I were engaged. I had worked all day and then went straight to my college classes. He was working a second shift at the time, so I knew I wouldn't get to see him that day. When I came out to the car after class, there was a card and my favorite Fannie May candies waiting.

Even though I didn't get to see him, it meant so much that he took time out to find my car in the lot and make sure there was something waiting for me when I came out.

Another year, my husband left notes around the house and sent me on a scavenger hunt to find several small gifts hidden throughout the house. I can't recall exactly what the gifts were, but it's the thought he put into it that I remember.

Probably the best Valentine's Day of all was my first as a new mom. Of course, I was busy and exhausted as all new moms are. My husband sent me to the bathroom where the room was full of lit candles and the tub was filled to the top with bubble bath and had rose petals sprinkled on top. I got the night off as he took care of the diapering and feeding and putting the baby to bed. It was wonderful. I felt appreciated and loved and got a much-needed break. He didn't buy anything extravagant—in fact, he said he stumped the clerk at the florist when he asked not for flowers, but just flower petals and she wasn't even sure what to charge him. It was a gift of thought and that's really the best kind of all.

Some of the many things to be thankful for

February 14, 2010

As the new year started, I began a practice I had originally started several years ago at the urging of my mother. She bought me a gratitude journal and each day I was supposed to write something I was thankful for. Most days, I had a list of several items. Over the years there have been busy times when I haven't kept up with it, but sometimes something (either small or very significant) will happen to make that feeling of gratefulness return.

I think parents of young children, especially, can find many things in their lives to be thankful for. And even when things are tough and it's hard to find that silver lining in your day or you're feeling frustrated, keeping a gratitude journal forces you to look at the blessings you have. So, since I decided to start my journal again, I thought I'd share something from each day of my entries.

Running water.
Five healthy boys.
Hot shower.
Little boys' toothless grins.
Kentucky Fried Chicken for dinner that I didn't have to cook.
That the boys have a dog to play with.
Snow.
Laughing together.

CARRIE STEINWEG

Weekends.
Sunshine.
A field trip with preschoolers.
The troops that ensure our freedom.
Listening to my boys play together.
Having a vehicle to get me from place to place.
Play dates.
A cup of hot chocolate.
My son making dinner for the family.
Sleeping in.
Listening to my son read to his little brother.
Popcorn and a movie.
Baking cookies with my youngest boy.
My parents.
Watching my youngest imitate his father.
Comfortable bed.
My son packing his own lunch.
That I don't have a unibrow or a mustache.
The comfortable slippers I got for Christmas.
An unsolicited hug from one of the boys.
A weekend getaway.
Watching the kids smile.
Being together.

An old shirt provides comfort

February 25, 2010

One night recently as I was getting ready for bed, I pulled out some warm flannel pants and a worn-out shirt that usually goes with it. I put it on maybe once a week.

I held it up to the light and noticed that the fabric was thinning in a spot on the back near the neck. It's obviously seen better days and normally, I'd just pitch it in the garbage, but somehow I can't. Not just yet.

The shirt is a three-quarter-sleeve jersey type, gray in the middle with the Purdue mascot with black sleeves. I can't even guess the age of it. We'll just call it vintage.

I got it many years ago when I was a teenager in a bag of hand-me-down clothes my older sister gave me. It was bunched in with some T-shirts that my brother-in-law, Jerry, must have grown tired of.

My big sister was a teenager when I was born and I was probably about 7 years old when she met Jerry. He quickly became part of the family and got along great with my two older brothers. He became just as much a big brother to me as they were. Pam and Jerry married when I was 12.

I always enjoyed being around them. I'd visit them for a weekend and my sister and I would bake cookies together and go shopping. I was beyond thrilled when my nephew was born and loved seeing how happy they were to be parents.

Then when I was expecting my first child, we got the devastating news that Jerry had been diagnosed with lung cancer. He was in his early 40s, a nonsmoker and had a 1-year-old son.

He was incredibly optimistic and did everything he could to fight the disease.

About 18 months after his diagnosis, he traveled to Mayo Clinic for an operation, but didn't survive it. Sometimes I still can't believe that he's no longer with us.

If he were still alive, Jerry would be turning 58 this week. It's been nearly 15 years since he died, but he's not forgotten. I still think about him and miss him. I still find myself talking—kind of praying—to him once in a while with the assumption that he's my guardian angel. One day recently I was scrambling around the house looking for a book and asking him to help me find it. It suddenly fell off the shelf right in front of me. I can't help but think he's watching over me in a moment like that.

My sister has since remarried to a wonderful guy. My nephew has grown up. He's driving now and will graduate high school next year. Even though he grew up without his father around him, I can sometimes catch something in his speech or mannerisms that reminds me so much of his dad.

I know it's just a piece of tattered cloth and it's time to get rid of it. I don't think I'll be wearing it anymore, but it still elicits good memories and I think it will have to stay in a drawer for a little while more just so I know it's there.

Children need several hugs a day

Sunday, March 28, 2010

We've long heard that an apple a day is a needed component for good health. Proper nutrition and good food choices should definitely be a priority. However, equally important to good overall health is the security, comfort and joy provided by a simple hug.

I grew up in an affectionate family. Whenever there was a family get-together, there were always hugs and kisses before parting. The final act before heading off to bed was a goodnight hug and kiss from Mom and Dad. Although it often just seemed routine, it was also meaningful and the day didn't feel complete if that bit of affection was missed.

Since I grew up that way, I just assumed as a child that all kids were showered with hugs by their family members. However, that's not the case.

It's something so simple, that reaps such great rewards, yet some parents don't give that simple bit of confidence and love to their children. And realistically, it's not just kids who need those hugs. No matter your age, that physical contact and connection with a human being is imperative for them to fully thrive.

Parents benefit as much as their children. Yet I know adults who grew up in homes were hugging was a rarity.

Noted author and family therapist Virginia Satir's recommendation was that we need four hugs a day for survival, eight hugs a day for maintenance and twelve hugs a day for growth.

I recall seeing a man named Juan Mann on "Oprah" who began a hugging campaign. He was adamant about the idea that everyone needed to be hugged, even if the hug came from a complete stranger. He stood on a busy street with a sign that read "Free Hugs" and while he came across more skeptics that willing participants, he knew that he had made a small difference to each person who accepted a hug. He encourages people to set out on their own hugging campaigns and reach out to strangers. You can find out more about his movement on **FREEHUGCAMPAIGN.COM**.

In a University of North Carolina study, hugs were shown to increase the bonding hormone oxytocin, which is present in breastfeeding women. It also showed a link between frequent hugging and a decreased risk of heart disease, lower blood pressure and a decrease in the stress hormone cortisol.

A study of a Korean orphanage revealed that babies who received 15 additional minutes of attention in the form of eye contact, voice and hugs gained more weight and had greater growth increases.

I could go on and on about the virtues and necessity of human contact, but I won't bore you with more statistics and studies.

Most people know that hugging is a good thing.

And following Satir's recommendation of a dozen hugs a day is doable. A dozen apples a day might not be so good.

Celebrate the joys of motherhood

May 9, 2010

When I glanced at the calendar and realized this column would run on Mother's Day, I wasn't sure what to write. In past years I've shared stories about my mom and about being a mom, so today I'm just throwing a few random Mom thoughts out there and wishing a happy day to all the moms I know!

* There are so many sappy and sentimental things to say about what it feels like to become a mom, but it can really not even be closely described in words and you just can't imagine the feeling until you're there.

* I'm so lucky to still have my mother with us. This August she'll turn 75 (Shh! Don't let her know I revealed her age.) I love her dearly and I've learned so many things from her over the years and am so happy that she's been here to get to know her grandchildren.

* I'm probably not the only person who has been cursed by her mother with "I hope you have one just like you!" Well, I can't say any of my boys are just like me, but I can assure you they've thrown sufficient challenges at me to fulfill that wish of revenge.

* Ugh! My mom told me this long ago and I should have listened. Write the names on the back of all the baby pictures because later on, you won't be able to tell them apart. Once again, she was right.

* Mother's Day isn't a happy time for everyone. I noticed a friend's Facebook status this week mentions how much it makes her miss

her mother who died many years ago. For those who have lost their mothers or who don't have good relationships with their mothers, the day can bring sadness and pain more than happiness. If you know a friend in this situation, send her a note to let you know you're thinking of her.

* I've had a lot of friends in my life who are old enough to be my mom and I've always admired them and valued their advice. I have to give a shout out to my former co-workers who have known me since I was a teen and remember some who are no longer with us—Jeanette Cobb, June Basiaga, Mary Ann Rush, Fran Saucier, Jeanine DesJardins, Alma Alexander, Barb Pavoni, Gladys Banke, Dee Degenhart, Lucille Baranowski and Estelle Surufka.

* The opinions of peers, friends and teachers are very important, but it's a parent's approval, opinion and acceptance that matters the most. I know there are days that I don't get it right, but I do my best to let them know they are loved no matter what.

* And some advice to any of the kids out there who don't know what to get for Mom. Do the dishes without asking, do some dusting, sweep the floor, clean your room or fill a bubble bath for her. On any other day, it might cause Mom to be suspicious about what you've been up to, but do it on Mother's Day and it'll earn your double brownie points.

Time marches on whether Mom wants it to or not

May 23, 2010

Sixteen years ago, I packed my bags to be at the hospital early in the morning to be induced with my first child. It was nearly two weeks past my due date and since there were no signs of labor, we had to move things along.

During pregnancy, you greatly anticipate the day of your baby's arrival and as the time gets closer you get anxious wondering what each day will bring.

You never know when a baby is ready to be born.

Sometimes they're early.

Sometimes they're late.

Sometimes they're right on time.

I remember that night and the uncertainty was gone. I knew that it was going to be the last night I would go to sleep not being a mother. I knew that once I got to the hospital, there was no turning back. The baby was going to be born. When I left the hospital, I would be a parent.

It was exciting and frightening all at the same time.

Ten-and-a-half hours after arriving at the hospital, I had a son. It was the most intense, exhausting and exhilarating day of my life.

After going hours without labor progressing, being prodded with a vacuum device and forceps, followed by well over an hour of pushing, my baby finally arrived.

He was healthy, but had swallowed some fluid and his first few days were spent in the neonatal unit. At 10 days old, we were finally able to bring him home.

Those early days and weeks seemed to move so slowly. It was an ongoing routine of feeding, burping and changing that was repeated every couple hours around the clock. I looked forward to each new milestone hoping he would soon be smiling, then rolling, then sitting, then crawling, then walking, then talking. Back then it seemed to take forever. Today, it seems that it all flashed by in the blink of an eye.

It's just so mind-boggling to believe that the little baby that I snuggled with has passed so many milestones and is nearly an adult. I once held him in one arm and now he's taller than I am.

Moms are often masters at organizing, managing and controlling things. But there are things that even Moms have no control over. You can't hold back time or growth. Time marches on even if we don't want it to. And most of the time, it moves faster than we'd prefer.

Would you like to see your manuscript become a book?

If you are interested in becoming a PublishAmerica author, please submit your manuscript for possible publication to us at:

acquisitions@publishamerica.com

You may also mail in your manuscript to:

**PublishAmerica
PO Box 151
Frederick, MD 21705**

www.publishamerica.com

CPSIA information can be obtained at www.ICGtesting.com
Printed in the USA
236546LV00001B/100/P